PROGRESSIVE CAPITALISM IN BRITAIN

This collection considers key issues in the progressive capitalism and inclusive prosperity debates, setting out a way forward for a new political economy in Britain. It is the result of collaboration between the Policy Network and IPPR thinktanks.

About Policy Network

Policy Network is an international thinktank and research institute. Its network spans national borders across Europe and the wider world with the aim of promoting the best progressive thinking on the major social and economic challenges of the 21st century.

Its work is driven by a network of politicians, policymakers, business leaders, public service professionals, and academic researchers who work on long-term issues relating to public policy, political economy, social attitudes, governance and international affairs. This is complemented by the expertise and research excellence of Policy Network's international team.

www.policy-network.net

About IPPR

IPPR is the UK's leading progressive thinktank. It is an independent registered charity with more than 40 staff members, paid interns and visiting fellows. Its main office is in London, with IPPR North, IPPR's dedicated thinktank for the north of England, operating out of offices in Newcastle and Manchester.

Its purpose is to conduct and publish research into, and promote public education in, the economic, social and political sciences, and in science and technology; including the effect of moral, social, political and scientific factors on public policy and on the living standards of all sections of the community.

www.ippr.org

PROGRESSIVE CAPITALISM IN BRITAIN

Pillars for a New Political Economy

Edited by Patrick Diamond, Tony Dolphin and Roger Liddle

policy network

IPPR

ROWMAN & LITTLEFIELD INTERNATIONAL

London • New York

Published by Rowman & Littlefield International, Ltd.
Unit A, Whitacre, 26-34 Stannary Street, London, SE11 4AB
www.rowmaninternational.com

Rowman & Littlefield International, Ltd. is an affiliate of Rowman & Littlefield
4501 Forbes Boulevard, Suite 200, Lanham, Maryland 20706, USA
With additional offices in Boulder, New York, Toronto (Canada), and Plymouth (UK)
www.rowman.com

British Library Cataloguing in Publication Information Available
A catalogue record for this book is available from the British Library

ISBN: PB 978-0-9928705-3-9

Library of Congress Cataloging-in-Publication Data

Progressive capitalism in Britain : pillars for a new political economy / edited by Patrick Diamond, Tony Dolphin and Roger Liddle.
pages cm
"This collection considers key issues in the progressive capitalism and inclusive prosperity debates, setting out a way forward for a new political economy in Britain. It is the result of collaboration between the Policy Network and IPPR think tanks"—Introduction.
ISBN 978-0-9928705-3-9 (pbk. : alk. paper) — ISBN 978-0-9928705-4-6 (electronic)
1. Great Britain—Economic policy—1997– 2. Capitalism—Great Britain. 3. Great Britain—Politics and government—2007– I. Diamond, Patrick, editor of compilation. II. Dolphin, Tony, editor of compilation. III. Liddle, Roger, editor of compilation. IV. Policy Network, issuing body. V. Institute for Public Policy Research (London, England) issuing body.
HC256.7.P76 2015
330.941—dc23
2015003877

∞™ The paper used in this publication meets the minimum requirements of American National Standard for Information Sciences Permanence of Paper for Printed Library Materials, ANSI/NISO Z39.48-1992.

Printed in the United States of America

CONTENTS

About the Contributors vii

Introduction 1
Tony Dolphin

A New Political Economy for Britain 5
David Sainsbury

The Smart State 11
Philippe Aghion

A Progressive Economic Strategy 17
Wendy Carlin

Putting in Place an Innovation System That Will Allow the UK to Compete in Global Markets 23

Equipping Young People with the Skills Employers Need 35

Reforming Corporate Governance to Encourage Long-Term Thinking and Investment 51

Developing a Financial System That Meets the Needs of the Rest of the Economy 65

The Political Challenge of Progressive Capitalism 79
Roger Liddle and Patrick Diamond

ABOUT THE CONTRIBUTORS

Philippe Aghion is Robert C. Waggoner Professor of Economics at Harvard University.

Wendy Carlin is professor of economics at University College London and research fellow of the Centre for Economic Policy Research.

Patrick Diamond is vice-chair of Policy Network and lecturer in public policy at Queen Mary, University of London.

Tony Dolphin is associate director for economic policy at IPPR.

Roger Liddle is chair of Policy Network and a member of the House of Lords.

David Sainsbury is a member of the House of Lords and a former minister for science and innovation. He is the author of *Progressive Capitalism: How to Achieve Economic Growth, Liberty and Social Justice* (2013).

INTRODUCTION

Tony Dolphin

Since the financial crisis and recession, there have been many lively debates about economic policy in the UK. Unsurprisingly, these initially centred on the appropriate response to the crisis, in terms of fiscal and monetary policy, bailing out the banks and ensuring that the financial system was put on a sounder footing. Subsequently, the debate has moved on to encompass, at various times, reducing unemployment, rebalancing the economy, cutting the government's deficit, reducing the size of the state and securing increases in living standards for all. There has been less debate, however, about the nature of the UK's political economy. This edited collection by IPPR and Policy Network aims to help fill this gap.

In the first chapter, David Sainsbury suggests that a new progressive political economy for the UK should be based on three principles. First, that institutions are crucial elements of a capitalist economy; second, that the state has to be involved in their design to resolve conflicts of interest and to ensure that public goods are provided; and third, that social justice – fairness – should be an important measure of economic performance. He argues that many of the UK's institutions needed reforming if the UK is to compete in a 'race to the top', with firms increasingly adopting a high value-added model, and that the government will have a big role to play in this process.

Huge changes are taking place in the global economy – globalisation and technological progress – meaning that what was appropriate 20 or 30 years ago might no longer be so. In chapter 2, Philippe Aghion picks up the first two of David Sainsbury's principles and argues that institutions and the role of the state have to evolve with the economy. While it was appropriate in the postwar era for the state to back national champions; attempt to smooth the business cycle through tax and spending policies; and run a welfare system that simply paid benefits and topped up low incomes, something different is now required. State investment has to be targeted in a pro-competition way that encourages innovation, rather than in a protectionist way; governments need to pay at least as much attention to the supply side of the economy as to the demand side; and welfare policies need to be based on the 'flexicurity' model.

In chapter 3, Wendy Carlin grapples with David Sainsbury's third principle: social justice (though she prefers to think in terms of reduced inequality rather than fairness). She argues that insufficient attention has been paid to the interconnectedness of rising inequality, central bank interest rate policy and weak investment in advanced countries, including the UK. She thinks that policies need to seek to secure more equal outcomes and that in a country that is already doing a lot of redistribution, such as the UK, policies need to address the market distribution of incomes and assets. This could encompass health and social care and education. She notes, however, that relatively low productivity growth in these sectors implies that their share in gross domestic product will increase and that being state-funded requires taxation to increase as a share of gross domestic product, too, which might prove to be a barrier.

Returning to institutions, four sets of institutions are likely to prove crucial to the performance of the economy: the national system of innovation; the education and training system; the institutions that underpin the governance of companies; and the financial system. Chapters 4 to 7 report discussions at four roundtable meetings convened during 2014 to develop ideas on how Britain's institutions need to evolve to support a new progressive capitalism. We would like to thank all the participants at these discussions, particularly those who agreed to make prepared statements. They were as follows:

On innovation: Lord Paul Drayson, Lee Hopley (EEF) and Professor Richard Jones (University of Sheffield).

On skills: Lord Kenneth Baker, Dr Hilary Steedman (London School of Economics) and Professor Lorna Unwin (Institute of Education).

On corporate governance: Sir George Cox (Shorts), Stephen Haddrill (Financial Reporting Council) and Deborah Hargreaves (High Pay Centre).

On finance: Anthony Browne (British Bankers Association), Cormac Hollingsworth (Social Market Foundation), Catherine Howarth (ShareAction) and Dr Paul Woolley (London School of Economics).

The discussions were rich ones and there was not complete agreement on the way forward in any area. But some strong conclusions did emerge. The government has a crucial role to play in supporting innovation-led growth through spending on research, providing finance for development and commercialisation, and bringing researchers and businesses together. The UK's vocational and education system needs to be reformed so that it is central to productivity advances and better designed to give young people the skills they need to thrive in the workforce. Shareholders need to be encouraged and supported to align the interests of managements with the long-term performance of their companies, rather than focusing on short-term results. And the government should use regulation to increase transparency within the financial sector to encourage it to deliver a better service to the rest of the economy.

Finally, in chapter 8, Roger Liddle and Patrick Diamond address some of the problems likely to be encountered in developing a new progressive political economy for the UK. In particular, they argue that it is crucial that business is seen to be part of the solution not part of the problem, which raises the tricky problem of how to secure the backing of businesses for a model of capitalism that requires significant changes in the way they behave. They call for the start of a dialogue between business and progressive thinkers about the way forward.

Leaving the UK's model of political economy unchanged is not an option in the modern global economy. The existing model has resulted in an unbalanced economy with relative low productivity and a structural balance of payments deficit. Without reform these problems will not go away, and indeed could worsen. A debate about what the new model should look like is overdue. This pamphlet is a contribution to that debate.

Tony Dolphin is associate director for economic policy at IPPR.

A NEW POLITICAL ECONOMY FOR BRITAIN

David Sainsbury

In a recent article in *Foreign Affairs*, entitled 'The Future of History', Francis Fukuyama pointed out that despite widespread anger at Wall Street bailouts, there has been no great upsurge of support for leftwing political parties. This lack of leftwing mobilisation he attributed, I believe rightly, to a failure in the realm of ideas. The financial crash of 2008 revealed major flaws in the neoliberal view of capitalism, and an objective view of the last 35 years shows that the British economy has not performed well compared with the previous 30 years in terms of economic growth, financial stability and social justice. But progressive political economists have not yet put forward a credible alternative. If you want to oppose a bad idea, you have to put forward a credible good one.

Progressive politicians and policymakers need, therefore, to debate what should be the outlines of a new progressive political economy, which is clearly different from the neoliberalism that has dominated political debate for the last 35 years, but which equally is not seen as a return to the failed policies of the 1960s and 1970s. A number of attempts have been made in recent years to describe such a political economy. We have had 'responsible capitalism', 'ethical capitalism' and 'moral capitalism'. But I do not think that any of them have either stated clearly what goals they are seeking to achieve or credibly described what role the state needs to play in order to achieve them. To say simply that one is in favour of responsible capitalism, ethical capitalism or moral capitalism does not advance the argument at all, as no one is arguing for irresponsible capitalism, unethical capitalism or immoral capitalism. It fails what the late Simon Hoggart called the law of the ridiculous reverse.

It might be argued that we do not need to have a view about political economy, that a pragmatic approach to policymaking is all that is needed for political success. I think to take this view is a mistake for two reasons. First, if a political party's programme of reform is going to attract voters, it must be able to state credibly how the state is going to achieve the party's goals. Second, if a political party does not state clearly what its political economy is, then it can be certain that its opponents will pin one on it that is politically disastrous.

A new progressive political economy must be based on a firm belief in capitalism – that is to say on an economic system in which most of the assets are privately owned and production is guided and income distributed largely through the operation of markets. But it must also incorporate three defining beliefs of progressive thinking: the crucial role of institutions; the need for the state to be involved in the design of institutions in order to resolve conflicting interests and provide public goods; and the use of social justice, defined as fairness, as an important measure of a country's economic performance.

It was a great mistake of neoclassical economists not to see that capitalism is a socio-economic system, and that institutions are an essential part of it. The financial crash of 2008 was made far worse by a number of institutional failures, such as the high level of leverage that banks were allowed to have. Endless empirical studies have shown that four institutions have a major impact on the performance of firms and, therefore, on a country's economic growth. These four institutions are the national system of innovation – that is, the network of institutions in the public and private sectors whose activities and interventions initiate and diffuse new technologies; a country's education and training system; the institutions that underpin the governance of firms; and the institutions that underpin financial markets. None of these institutions are today performing their function in the UK economy as well as they should, and they need to be reformed.

The second defining belief of progressive thinking is that the state has to be involved in the design and reform of a country's institutions. Institutions do not evolve spontaneously as neoliberals believe. The state has to be involved because in the case of the institutions that underpin labour and financial markets and corporate governance it has to resolve the conflicting interests of participants. In the case of a country's education and training system and its national system of innovation, they are largely public goods, which have to be provided by the state. Politicians, however, should be careful about trying to cherry-pick the economic institutions of a different variety of capitalism. At first sight it may seem very sensible, for example, for a country like the UK to try to copy the successful technical training system of a country like Germany, but all the evidence shows that such a policy is likely to fail.

The reason why the different institutional forms of capitalism are not scattered randomly across countries, and why some countries have more market-based institutions and others have more non-market based ones, lies in the complementarities that exist between different types of institutions. Technical education in Germany depends to a considerable extent on coordination across firms in an industry, which, in Germany, is achieved by industry associations and trade unions supervising a publicly subsidised training system. This system cannot be transferred easily to the UK because we do not have strong industry associations and trade unions which could deliver such a training system, and we have, therefore, to find our own institutional solution.

Attempts by some countries to switch to another variety of capitalism have also demonstrated that it is an extremely difficult thing to do unless there is huge political commitment. The most explicit attempt to switch to another variety – that of French governments to create a German-style coordinated market economy in France between the mid-1980s and the mid-1990s – was a complete failure. Finally, it is not clear that over the long term there is a systematic variation in the economic performance of the two main varieties of capitalism: liberal market economies and coordinated market economies.

I think it is important at this stage of the argument to understand that the role of the state that I have been describing is an enabling or market-supporting one. It is not the command-and-control role promoted by traditional socialists or the minimalist role of neoliberals.

The third defining belief of progressive thinking is that social justice needs to be used as an important measure of a country's economic performance. Neoliberals assess the economic performance of a country solely in terms of economic growth and freedom. But if one is concerned with the wellbeing of society, I do not think it is possible to argue that a wealthy society with most of its wealth held by the top 1 per cent is better than a slightly less wealthy society with its wealth more evenly spread. I also believe that fairness is a better measure of social justice than equality. It is difficult to devise practical and effective policies to achieve equality in a market economy, because there is a real trade-off between equality and economic growth, and because egalitarianism is not a popular policy even for many low-income people. In my experience, trade unions are much more interested in differentials than in a simple policy of equality of pay for all. It is not, however, too difficult to think of policies that will create a fairer economy by preventing the appropriation of wealth by the directors of companies and investment managers, by raising the minimum wage, and by creating in the UK an effective system of technical education to provide the technicians industry so badly needs.

These are the outlines of what I believe a new progressive political economy should look like, and which I have described in my book *Progressive Capitalism*. I also believe that western governments that do not adopt it, and instead continue to cling to a neoliberal political economy, will find it difficult to grow their economies in the new global economy in which they find themselves. In the new global economy, which is awash with cheap labour, we will not be able to compete if we 'race to the bottom', with firms competing by seeking ever-cheaper labour, land and capital, and countries competing by deregulating and shrinking social benefits. We also will not be able to produce the good quality jobs we desperately need: jobs with hours and pay that lift families out of poverty, and provide opportunities for training and promotion.

The only way we will be able to compete, improve our standard of living and create good quality jobs is by seeing ourselves as being involved in a 'race to the top', with firms improving their value-added by innovation in existing industries, and by developing the capability to compete in new and more sophisticated industries, where value-added is generally higher. Firms will only be able to do this if governments abandon the neoliberal political economy, which is based on a firm belief that governments have no role to play in the economy, and replace it with a new progressive political economy – progressive capitalism – that sees the state as having a key role to play in providing the conditions that enable dynamic companies to innovate and grow.

David Sainsbury is a member of the House of Lords and a former minister for science and innovation. He is the author of *Progressive Capitalism: How to Achieve Economic Growth, Liberty and Social Justice* (2013).

THE SMART STATE

Philippe Aghion

Post-second world war European economic and welfare policies had three main pillars. The first was a top-down industrial policy based on national champions and state-owned firms. The second was a Keynesian macroeconomic policy to smooth the business cycle: essentially, whenever there was a recession government would spend more or cut taxes in order to boost consumption, relying on the so-called 'Keynesian multiplier' to boost growth. The third pillar was the welfare system which paid various forms of benefits and credits to top-up low salaries or to enable people to have access to various services that they would not otherwise have had.

This set of policies was very well adapted to the type of catch-up economy that existed in the postwar years, where growth was based on copying and adapting the more advanced technologies and techniques of wealthier economies, particularly the US. However, the rules of the game have now changed. European states no longer exist in a relatively closed, protectionist, and less globalised era.

COMING TO TERMS WITH THE NEW ECONOMIC ENVIRONMENT

European states have caught up with the leading economies and, under pressure from the new emerging economies that are also doing some catching up of their own, have to rely on innovation. European economies can no longer just be imitators; they have to be innovators.

Globalisation has forced states to deliver more and more innovation-led growth. However, innovation-led growth has also undermined the very foundations on which economic and welfare policies have been built. In the innovation economy, Schumpeterian creative destruction means the old model of industrial policy based on national champions and state-owned firms is obsolete because greater competition means that new firms are constantly destroying and replacing old firms. This competition is crucial for the innovation process. Indeed, it is a catalyst for innovation when an economy is at the frontier of production possibilities. The consequence is that states can no longer rely on old-fashioned, top-down *Colbertiste* industrial policy.

Further, the nature of an open and global economy means that governments can no longer just decide to increase domestic growth by boosting consumer demand because increased demand may well end up being for foreign products, particularly those that are either better quality or less expensive than domestically produced products. States must, therefore, ensure they are competitive.

This means that states can no longer just have a demand-side approach; they also need a supply-side approach. We can no longer only have automatic stabilisers for consumers; we must also have them for firms, to make sure that firms, particularly those that are credit constrained, can maintain their R&D investment over the business cycle. Instead of a Keynesian macroeconomic policy focused entirely on the demand side, we must, therefore, develop a counter-cyclical macroeconomic policy that also helps firms maintain their R&D, employee 'upskilling' and other kinds of growth-enhancing investments.

There must be a new social role for the state, too. Creative destruction means there is a perpetual cycle of job creation and destruction. The new state must be there to help by providing the unemployed with good income insurance and good training so that workers can bounce from one job to another. This role has in the past been fulfilled by trade unions and employers but the new economy will require a more advanced model of 'flexicurity'. Denmark, where they have flexibility in hiring and firing on the firm side, although there is also income insurance and facilities for workers to retrain and find a new job, is a good example of this concept. Firms are penalised if they abuse the system, workers are penalised if they do not actively retrain for a new job or if they refuse the new jobs that are offered to them, and the state co-finances the system, which in turn supports innovation-led growth.

WHAT PROGRESSIVE GOVERNMENTS HAVE TO DO

Governments have to do three things: they need to promote growth; they need to make sure that growth is inclusive and socially just; and they need to reduce budget deficits. But how can they do these three things together?

First, it is high time to depart from the old Keynesian view that governments can invest in all things everywhere. State investments need to be targeted. This targeting can be done in two forms: horizontal targeting, by which we mean investments, such as education, research, and support to innovating small and medium-sized enterprises, which benefit all sectors of the economy. Then there is vertical targeting: support that is focused on priority sectors (for example, renewable energies, biotech, and health). However, if states do sectoral policy, they cannot do it the old way. It has to be a pro-competition sectoral policy, not one of sheltered protectionism. States can promote competition, for example, by making firms compete for state subsidies.

Crucially, to do this, states must ensure that their investments are well governed and produce tangible results. Therefore, subsidies to universities or schools must go along with good governance of these institutions. Similarly, subsidies to particular sectors must be designed and governed so that they do not prevent competition and so that the state can exit from projects that turn out to be non-performing.

If progressives want to achieve inclusive growth while still respecting budgetary discipline, then two evils must be avoided. One is what I call 'primitive Keynesianism' – the idea that demand drives growth, that the only thing that matters is for governments to spend and that, therefore, the supply side does not matter. This is not to say that automatic stabilisers are not important, but we cannot just dismiss the supply side either.

The second evil is what I call the 'tax-and-spend' philosophy – the idea that governments can tax as much as they want, without any negative effect on innovation and growth, especially if part of the tax revenues are used as public subsidies. For example, in France, François Hollande introduced a 75 per cent tax in the belief that taxation either would be neutral or would have its effects offset by the establishment of a *Banque Publique d'Investissement*. This has proved very wrong, as shown by the decline in private investment and job creation in France in the last few years.

The best example of a country that got this right is Sweden. Until the early 1990s Sweden had labour income tax rates of up to 90 per cent and capital taxation with an upper rate of 80 per cent. The result was major capital flight and a serious decline in incentives. In 1991, following the Swedish banking crisis, the government introduced a series of reforms, reducing the maximum marginal tax rate on labour to 57 per cent and making the tax on capital income a flat rate of 30 per cent. The changes had a huge effect in fostering growth and innovation. The rate of patenting increased by 250 per cent and growth increased accordingly, while public spending was actually reduced as a share in gross domestic product. Yet these changes were achieved while maintaining progressivity – Sweden is still the second most equal society in the world (behind Denmark). Sweden attracts foreign investments in spite of its still progressive taxation system because it offers an exceptional environment in terms of public infrastructure and human capital.

The Swedish case also demonstrates that, when reducing budget deficits, states cannot rely solely on increasing taxation, but rather should use a mixture of tax reform and public spending reform. That the latter course of action is likely to be more growth-enhancing than the former has been demonstrated in recent empirical work by Alberto Alesina, Silvia Ardagna and Francesco Giavazzi. In particular, taxing too much has a discouraging effect on consumption and on firms' investment, and can also end up reducing tax revenues.

The policy that works best is thus a mixture of targeted reductions in spending, combined with some tax increases and the rationalisation of the tax system. This is what we can call the smart state – neither the old welfare state of the left nor the minimalist state of the right.

In this era of globalisation, economic trends show that state intervention in the economy is warranted. But state intervention cannot be like it used to be. It has to be a smart state where governments select their sectors, they select their areas of intervention and they make sure that good governance goes with state investments so that the investments are as cost effective as they can be. This is the role of the state in the growth process.

Philippe Aghion is Robert C. Waggoner Professor of Economics at Harvard University.

A PROGRESSIVE ECONOMIC STRATEGY

Wendy Carlin

The last five years have transformed the way we think about short- and longer-run economic strategy. Short-term strategy focuses on creating high levels of employment consistent with stable inflation, along with a sustainable external balance and public debt ratio. Longer-term strategy addresses the goals of improving environmentally sustainable living standards and providing opportunities for people with all kinds of talents to have satisfying working lives. This chapter concentrates on the latter – particularly the inter-connected issues of innovation, redistribution and labour-absorbing services – but begins with the former.

LESSONS FROM THE 'GREAT MODERATION'

From a world in which the problems of stabilisation policy seemed to have been solved, government debt ratios were falling and poor countries were catching up with the rich, we have moved to a world in which households now face increased uncertainty about jobs and incomes, are burdened with debt in many countries and the ability of the state to intervene creatively appears heavily circumscribed. In between the two phases was a brief moment when governments acted in a coordinated way to avert disaster and public confidence in the constructive role of government increased.

The years of crisis and recession have led to a much more critical appraisal of the achievements of the 'Great Moderation'. It is clear that in many countries high growth was not based on improved long-run prospects for the economy. In some, like Spain, Ireland and the UK, it was based on unsustainable patterns of demand underpinned by appreciated real exchange rates, which artificially boosted real wages and allowed high employment to be maintained consistent with low consumer price inflation. In these cases, buoyant growth was sustained by rising levels of private debt; elsewhere growth was supported by rising public debt.

In another group of countries, a different pattern developed. In Germany, depressed demand at home and dependence on export markets for growth promoted supply-side restructuring by the private sector. But as the fiscal position improved, the opportunity to implement reforms that would have set in place a more balanced growth model was not taken. As a result, the divergent patterns and associated growing imbalances across countries were reinforced.

It was possible for central banks to achieve successful inflation targeting consistent with the build-up of the major imbalances that eventually produced both the crisis and the particular shape of the post-crisis recession. The institutions of the liberalised financial sector took advantage of incentives to increase their leverage in what was widely viewed as a lower-risk environment. This created the conditions for a financial crisis when the assessment of risk reversed. However, an under-explored aspect of the build-up to the crisis is the interconnection of central bank interest rate policy, rising inequality and weak investment (outside housing) in the advanced economies.

Patterns of increased inequality varied a lot across countries in timing and intensity during the decades preceding the crisis. Common factors behind rising wage inequality included globalisation and technical progress biased towards more highly educated workers. The weakening of unions was more important in some countries than in others.

A related development was an increased profit share at the expense of wages. But little attention was paid to why the high and rising profits of the non-financial sector were not showing up in higher fixed investment. Central banks simply kept interest rates low to support demand and maintain inflation close to target through the extension of loans to ever less creditworthy households, with houses (although not in the UK, where they are needed) rather than new factories or workplaces being built.

One problem for progressive economic policy is to engage with the causes of the lack of dynamism in the non-financial business sector before the crisis. Businesses were awash with profits they did not invest. Opinions differ widely about the potential for new technologies to drive a revival of investment. Unlike in the 1930s, there does not seem such an obvious set of new general purpose technologies (based on electrification at that time) that could form the basis of renewed capital accumulation in the advanced economies.

Higher inequality and profits seem not to have had their expected payoff in terms of more risk-taking by entrepreneurs in the non-financial sector that would lead to investment in new capacity in the advanced countries, producing new products with lower-cost production processes.

INEQUALITY AND THE ROLE OF ECONOMIC POLICY IN SUPPORTING EGALITARIAN INTERVENTIONS

There has been recent debate in the UK about the balance between policies that support a reduction in inequality by interventions affecting the market distribution – or 'predistribution' – of incomes and assets itself or affecting the post-tax-and-transfer distribution. Most of the discussion has been about income, but one of the most obvious predistribution interventions on the asset side is to raise human capital among poor households. Education policies in the Nordic countries have contributed to the relatively egalitarian market distribution of income. The challenge is that both the education policies and any substantial post-tax-and-transfer redistribution require political consent for high taxes.

There is a great variety among rich countries in both the primary distribution of income and in the post-tax-and-transfer distribution. An important but insufficiently emphasised point is that countries with egalitarian post-tax-and-transfer distributions compete successfully in a globalised world. Three of the six countries (four Nordic countries plus Austria and Belgium) with low post-tax-and-transfer inequality have market distributions less equal than the median among 21 major economies and three have market distributions that are more equal than the median. Korea has the most egalitarian market distribution and almost no redistribution via taxes and transfers, which means it ends up just below the median in terms of post-tax-and-transfer equality. The UK is one of the most unequal economies in terms of the market distribution (second bottom) and yet at number 10 in terms of the extent of redistribution. This still leaves it in the bottom five of 21 countries for post-tax-and-transfer equality.

What does this imply? Especially in countries with high disposable income inequality and that are already doing a lot of redistribution like the UK, the palette of egalitarian policies should be extended to include the market distribution. Since people think that they deserve their market incomes, attacking inequality through selective policies of asset redistribution that are consistent with widely held norms may incur less political resistance. Examples are policies that fall under the 'levelling the playing field' rubric, such as health and social care, schooling for all and bequest taxation. Also, measures that target the market distribution of income directly – such as eradicating discrimination in labour markets and wage compression – are likely to have more political support than measures that try to affect the post-tax-and-transfer distribution.

THE IMPLICATIONS FOR POLICY OF LABOUR-ABSORBING SERVICES IN THE ECONOMY

Progressive economic policy thinking also needs to grapple with the implications of relatively low productivity growth in tax-funded sectors of the economy. If productivity growth in the important service sectors of health, personal (elderly) care, and education is systematically slower than elsewhere in the economy, then the relative price of these services will go up. In the American economist William Baumol's original example, the relative price of a live performance of a Mozart quartet goes up as productivity improves elsewhere in the economy. The quartet still requires four people and 20 minutes as the centuries go by, but the number of minutes of work a concert-goer has to do to pay for a performance goes down. The benefits from the productivity growth in the dynamic sectors of the economy allow us to enjoy more live concerts and better health care as well as more manufactured goods or leisure.

A logical consequence of the existence of sectors with relatively low productivity growth (Baumol's 'stagnant services') is that their share in employment and in gross domestic product goes up. This is simply a feature of the characteristics of technology and preferences rather than efficiency. A better way of referring to the stagnant services is therefore as 'labour-absorbing' sectors. If the political challenges are won, sectors such as care and early childhood education could offer large and growing amounts of employment and decent jobs.

Baumol's 'cost disease' has important implications for the financing of public services. It predicts a rising share of the labour-absorbing sectors in GDP. Properly interpreted this is an indicator of the success of the capitalist economy in driving up productivity growth in other sectors. But if the labour-absorbing sectors are financed through taxation, a higher tax burden is inevitable. Again, this is a sign of success, not failure, of the economy – the higher tax burden is paid for by the higher market incomes that come from the higher productivity growth elsewhere.

A thriving dynamic sector of the economy is therefore crucial to provide the resources for high-quality, labour-absorbing sectors. One way of looking at the challenges for a progressive economic strategy is to see the complementarity among policies that boost innovation, reduce inequality in assets and in market income, and foster the growth of good jobs in the labour-absorbing service sectors.

Wendy Carlin is professor of economics at University College London and research fellow of the Centre for Economic Policy Research.

* This chapter is an extract from a 2012 Policy Network paper by Wendy Carlin entitled 'A Progressive Economic Strategy: Innovation, Redistribution and Labour-absorbing Services.'

PUTTING IN PLACE AN INNOVATION SYSTEM THAT WILL ALLOW THE UK TO COMPETE IN GLOBAL MARKETS

THE CASE FOR REFORM AND THE DIRECTION IT SHOULD TAKE

It is important first to understand why science and innovation are crucial to our economic future. Today all countries are involved in what is best described as a 'race to the top'. As a result of the collapse of communism, China's shift to a market economy and India's dismantling of its command-and-control economy, 1.5 billion new low-paid workers entered the world's labour market, almost exactly doubling it. The only way that developed countries can compete is by getting out of low value-added industries that are labour intensive and do not require highly skilled workers, such as cheap textiles, and getting into high value-added ones where innovation is of critical importance and which require a highly skilled workforce, areas such as the IT industry, aerospace and pharmaceuticals; hence the importance of science, technology and innovation.

The ability of companies to go into higher value-added areas depends very much on the institutions in their home country, in particular the country's 'national system of innovation': the network of institutions in the public and private sectors whose activities and interventions initiate and diffuse new technology. Thomas Friedman argued in his book *The World Is Flat* that because of the advance of information communication technologies people anywhere in the world can innovate and compete on equal terms. But as far as innovation is concerned, the world is very spiky. Innovation is concentrated to an extraordinary extent in places like Silicon Valley, Bangalore and Cambridge, England, where the institutions are supportive of it.

It is vitally important not to take the 'ground zero' approach chosen by too many parties in opposition. This consists in saying that all the current policies are wrong, and that only a radical overhaul of everything will bring success. This is disastrous because good policies get swept away with bad policies, introducing new policies and getting them to work takes time, and in the meantime the performance of companies suffer. This point will be of particular importance at the next general election because the last Labour government introduced a whole range of policies in the field of science and innovation, such as, for example, the Technology Strategy Board (now Innovate UK), the Higher Education Innovation Fund, R&D tax credits, the Small Business Research Initiative and the patent box. These have been largely successful, and to its great credit the coalition government has maintained them. As a result, UK industry and science have experienced 15 years of stable and consistent policies, the value of which cannot be overestimated.

Where, then, should the next government focus its efforts? There are three areas where action is required. First, we need a new 10-year plan for the funding of science that sees a steady increase in the amount allocated to basic research and also restores a stream of capital spending. If research councils and other funding bodies are able to plan ahead, resources are used much more efficiently. And while it probably made sense to cut back on capital spending if cuts had to be made in a period of austerity, if a stream of capital funding is not restored soon, the lack of modern facilities will start to impact the quality of science done.

Second, a major achievement of the last Labour government was to greatly improve the amount of knowledge transfer from universities to industry, mainly due to the Higher Education Innovation Fund. As a result, the amount of knowledge transfer from our universities is now in most cases as good as that of American universities. But more could be done to improve the commercialisations of research. More money should be allocated to Innovate UK (the new name for the Technology Strategy Board) for the setting-up of innovation platforms. By bringing together organisations focused on a particular social challenge such as intelligent transport systems and services, assisted living or low-carbon vehicles, innovation platforms enable the integration of a range of technologies along with better coordination of policy, regulations, standards and procurement. And there are plenty more areas where they could be put in place to help with the commercialisation of new technologies. The amount of money going to Innovate UK for generic technologies in order to narrow the 'valley of death' faced by small high-tech companies should also be increased.

To help with the process of commercialisation of research, the R&D expenditures of government departments, which have been run down by the coalition government in recent years, should be re-established, ring-fenced and used more effectively to support innovation in the industries that government departments sponsor. A striking feature of the US national system of innovation is the way that government departments use targeted resources of scientific and technological research to advance new technologies in the business community, whereas in the UK there have only been a few attempts, such as the creation of the Office for the Strategic Coordination of Health Research by the Department of Health and the support given by the Ministry of Defence to its contractors, to use government funds for innovation in industry. There are a number of areas such as energy, water and the agri-food industries that make an important contribution to UK industry, and which could benefit massively from government departments supporting innovation in them.

The third area where a future government should focus its efforts is the technological dimension of regional policy. There is an urgent need to support the growth of new industries in the poorer regions of the UK. The abolition, rather than reform, of the Regional Development Agencies was a mistake, and the Regional Growth Fund has achieved very little. We need to find a way, possibly through city deals, to support high-tech clusters in the regions and to implement the recommendations in Andrew Witty's excellent report, *Encouraging a British Invention Revolution*, on the role that universities can play in supporting new industries in the knowledge economy.

If political parties want to win the votes of industrialists and scientists, these are the sort of policies, which are focused and address clear weaknesses in our national system of innovation, that they should support.

FURTHER DISCUSSION OF WHAT NEEDS TO BE DONE

The UK needs to develop more clusters of industries where innovation thrives, creating productivity advantages that are hard to replicate in other countries and allowing high real wages to be paid. This will also help to rebalance the economy. Successful innovation leads to products that can be exported and investment spending to increase productive capacity.

At the moment, though, the UK is lagging behind its competitors. Spending on R&D, as a share of gross domestic product, in the UK in 2012 was below the average level of spending across the EU, and well below levels in countries like Germany and Sweden. This can be explained by three factors. First, excessive short-termism in business attitudes has led to a low level of investment spending in general. Second, the UK has gone further than most developed countries in increasing the share of services in its economy, at the expense of manufacturing. As a result, some of the big companies in the manufacturing sector that were traditionally more likely to engage in R&D no longer exist. Third, the level of foreign ownership of British industry is high. Firms generally prefer to do their research and development in their home country. Increasing R&D spending will, therefore, be difficult and it is imperative that the government plays a prominent role.

The last Labour government introduced a number of measures designed to support science and innovation, and most have been retained, or in some cases added to, by the coalition government. Entrepreneurs believe that, overall, these measures have been successful in promoting innovation. Future efforts should, therefore, build on them as far as possible. By adopting an evolutionary rather than revolutionary approach, government can provide a welcome element of stability.

The government should concentrate its effort to support innovation further on two broad areas: funding for basic and applied scientific research and improving the commercialisation of research. In doing so, it should also seek to ensure innovation is spread across the whole country.

Funding Basic Scientific Research

A key role for government is the funding of basic scientific research. If the UK is to develop new industrial strengths so that it can compete in the international market for high value-added goods, then maintaining a high level of scientific research is essential. This type of research is a public good – its benefits are enjoyed beyond those conducting the research – and it would not be provided by the private sector. It can, however, generate additional private sector activity. High-quality scientific research attracts entrepreneurs and businesses to locate near where it is taking place, so that their staff can more easily collaborate with researchers and identify commercial opportunities that can be exploited. The UK's science base is world-class. Its leading universities are held in high esteem around the world and, if they are resourced adequately, are well placed to attract such activity.

The government's science budget has been protected from cash cuts during the current parliament, but this will translate into a reduction of around one tenth in real terms. There will be more cuts to public spending in the next parliament, so freezing the science budget in nominal terms for another five years is likely to be a relatively generous settlement. However, if this happened, by 2020 government spending on science would have been cut by a fifth in the space of 10 years. This would be a blow to the chances of an innovation-led boost to the UK's productivity and its ability to grow and compete in world markets.

Government spending on science is not just vital because the type of research it funds would not otherwise happen; it also 'crowds in' complementary private sector spending. The loss of resources for innovation from a further squeeze on real spending is, therefore, greater than the cut to public spending alone. Even if it means larger cuts elsewhere, the next government should commit to holding the budget for current spending on science constant in real terms throughout the next parliament and announce its intention to allow increases in real terms in the following parliament (by which time it is to be hoped that the need for spending cuts will be in the past). To justify this commitment, the government should provide evidence of how much private sector spending has been boosted by extra public spending. It should also commit to increase the level of capital spending on science in real terms throughout the next 10 years, before a lack of modern facilities begins to have an effect on the quality of research.

Supporting Applied Research

The government supports applied research through Innovate UK, which brings researchers and businesses together to conduct research with specific commercial goals in mind and provides some financial support for their efforts. Most of these projects would not be undertaken without Innovate UK's support, and evaluations show high rates of return on completed projects. As any business would seek to expand its efforts in an area that produces high returns, so the government needs to find a way to increase the scale of the Innovate UK's activities.

The government also supports applied research indirectly through tax credits for R&D spending, which were introduced for small and medium-sized firms in 2000 and extended to include larger firms in 2002. Evidence from other developed economies suggested that tax credits would be successful in increasing the level of R&D spending in the UK, and this appears to have been the case. While there is undoubtedly some 'dead-weight' cost associated with them, they do incentivise investment spending.

It is also important that the government does what it can to protect the UK's existing research and development capabilities. Multinational companies tend to conduct most research and development in their home countries. There is a risk, therefore, that foreign takeovers of UK companies will lead to a reduction in the country's R&D capacity. Since this is undesirable from the national perspective, a public interest test should be applied to foreign takeovers in order to ensure that they do not result in a significant drop-off in R&D expenditure in the UK.

Venture capital is not a big source of finance for innovation in the UK and what support there is tends to be very concentrated in London and the south-east. More money is not forthcoming from venture capitalists because risk-adjusted prospective returns are not high enough. By increasing its own backing for R&D spending, the government can help to lower the risks for venture capitalists. It should also consult with leaders in the venture capital industry about changes to the tax system that would encourage greater backing for innovation spending. More generally, tax reform in the UK should reward (or at least reduce the tax burden on) long-term investment in the real economy and increase tax on activities that are designed to extract wealth from other parts of the economy, rather than to create value. A specific example of the former might be a graduated capital gains tax, with the rate payable reducing as the time period over which the gain is made increases.

However, although these steps will help at the margin, they are unlikely to be sufficient to offset the strong tendency among venture capitalists to want to see returns within a few years. It is unlikely they will ever develop the long-term thinking necessary to back major innovation projects that might take a decade or more to come to fruition and start to deliver a return to investors. In other countries, finance for such programmes is often provided by a state investment bank (for example, the KfW in Germany) or by public agencies (for example, the Defense Advanced Research Project Agency in the US).

The UK could learn from both models, which are superior ways of encouraging long-term innovation than tax breaks for Enterprise Investment Schemes and Venture Capital Trusts, and adopt either, or a mix of the two. More important than the specific institutional solution is the need to recognise that there is no form of private capital that will back the development of new technologies in their very early stages. The risks and uncertainties are just too great. Government has to provide the funding. Inevitably, though, not every venture that it supports will be successful.

Improving the Commercialisation of Research

The government can also play an important role in improving the commercialisation of research by building on existing initiatives to strengthen links between research bodies and businesses. Knowledge transfer is an essential element in any successful innovation system and it can be greatly facilitated by government. The most long-lasting initiatives are likely to be those that create partnerships and joint projects, such as joint procurement bids and coordinated research activities. At its simplest, this can just mean bringing together the right mix of researchers and businesses, as Innovate UK does with knowledge transfer networks. More substantially, the Higher Education Innovation Fund provides an incentive for universities to translate the results of their research efforts into industry and society. Since it was established, there has been a significant increase in knowledge transfer and the number of spin-off companies created.

Catapult centres – an elite network of technology and innovation centres – have successfully removed barriers and brought together researchers and businesses to develop new ideas and to commercialise them. They are a good example of how government support can help to promote networks and collaboration, leading to greater innovation. However, they are badly underfunded. They should be made a permanent feature of the UK's industrial landscape and the government should make more resources available to them. The length of time that the government has promised to give financial support to existing centres should be extended, recognising that successful research requires a long-term commitment, and more new Catapults should be established, centred on areas of research excellence in Britain's universities.

Innovation in the UK is currently very concentrated in some parts of the country, usually where there is a supportive institution. The government needs to promote innovation and the development of nascent industrial clusters across the whole country, and particularly in areas that have been worst hit by the effects of globalisation and technological change. One way to do this is through universities, which should become centres of economic development. The government should follow the recommendations made to it by Andrew Witty and put in place a set of incentives to encourage universities to focus more on commercialising the innovations of their researchers.

Universities are not fully geared up to exploit the UK's world-class science base. The idea that research should lead to wealth is absent from too many universities' thinking. Facilitating growth should become a 'third mission' for universities, along with teaching and research. The transfer of ideas from universities to business is still a marginal activity for most universities. A change of culture is needed and universities should be encouraged to increase the level of knowledge transfer between themselves and businesses, but in a way that does not undermine their research efforts. They should work with small and medium-sized firms to develop and commercialise technologies and report regularly to government on barriers to this activity and what needs to be done to remove them.

Where universities are engaged in knowledge transfer, their desire to hold onto a large share of the intellectual property in any new idea can in some cases be a barrier to effective knowledge transfer. Entrepreneurs will only start up new companies if they feel the potential rewards justify the uncertainties and risks. This may not be the case if they own insufficient intellectual property. In return for retaining less intellectual property, universities should be prepared to accept a 'golden share' in start-ups: a percentage of equity in the firm that cannot be diluted.

Some funding from government should be conditional on universities' innovation record. To help facilitate an increase in knowledge transfer, Witty suggested the government should make available funding of at least £1bn over the next five years for collaborative projects between universities and private firms to develop new technologies that will give the UK a comparative advantage in international markets. And it should increase to £250m a year the budget for Higher Education Innovation Funding, with a requirement that universities seek out innovative and potentially innovative small and medium-sized firms.

Encouraging Innovation to Tackle 'Big Challenges'

In general, government money to increase the commercialisation of research is best spent when it is used to back the search for solutions to specific problems, rather than when it supports particular technologies or ideas. This approach is also more likely to attract public backing. People understand the need to invest, for example, to find a solution to climate change and to tackle infectious diseases.

Innovation tends to occur in clusters. One successful advance solves a problem faced by society or meets the needs of customers, but in doing so creates new problems or needs, which in turn inspire further innovation. This clustering of innovation means the government is likely to get the biggest returns by focusing its resources in specific areas or, more particularly, on 'big challenges'. One obvious problem to focus on is the need to tackle climate change and make growth more 'green'. In part, this is about developing cleaner sources of energy, but the green agenda is actually much broader, involving, for example, cutting pollution, reducing resource use through energy efficiency and increasing recycling and the reuse of materials. At its most ambitious, a move to green growth would involve a major transformation of the economy.

Innovate UK should be given more funds to set up innovation platforms. These would bring together universities, companies and other organisations to tackle some of the challenges facing the UK today, including the move to green growth. Collaboration between the public and private sector in this way also ensures that policy, regulation and standards develop alongside technological advances, rather than being a barrier to them.

In other countries, including the US, government departments and agencies spend large sums of money on the development of new technologies and there is plenty of evidence that this leads to additional spending by the private sector. Traditionally, the state in the UK has done less. The government should increase the R&D budgets of government departments, which have been cut back over the last five years, and ensure they are used to support innovation in the industries that government departments sponsor.

Government departments should also make greater use of their procurement programmes to boost innovation. Instead of setting out detailed requirements when procuring goods and services, departments should be more inclined to specify the outcomes that they are seeking to achieve and to invite bidders to come up with solutions. In many cases, these might best be based on traditional ways of doing things, but, in some, more innovative solutions might be found that produce better outcomes, or similar outcomes at lower cost. Furthermore, to enable innovative small firms to bid for business, large contracts should be broken down into component parts.

CONCLUSION

The UK has too few industrial strengths and it cannot guarantee keeping those that it currently has. In the modern global economy, there is no such thing as a long-term sustainable competitive advantage. Firms and economies need to keep reinventing themselves and their products and services through innovation. UK spending in this area is insufficient and it needs to do more innovation so that it can develop more high value-added industries that can compete in global markets.

The government has crucial roles to play; innovation-led growth requires active state involvement. Government spending on basic and applied research encourages more spending by the private sector; the government can provide stable, long-term finance for the development of new technologies and their commercialisation; and it is uniquely well placed to bring together researchers and businesses. It needs to do more on all three fronts.

EQUIPPING YOUNG PEOPLE WITH THE SKILLS EMPLOYERS NEED

THE CASE FOR REFORM AND THE DIRECTION IT SHOULD TAKE

The first thing to do when looking at the reform of any institution is to be clear about what function it is expected to perform. It might be thought that it would be easy to state what function we want the education and training system of our country to perform, but it turns out that there is a wide range of views on its purpose. There are many teachers and educationalists who believe that the main aim of schools and universities should be to enable children to 'realise their potential' as individuals in some unspecified way, and that it is not to produce, as they would describe it, 'fodder for industry'. In this world, careers advice and the supply of labour market information to inform young people's educational choices are of little importance, and what proportion of young people take which subject at school and university is not of much interest.

However, work is central to most people's lives, and if they are to lead fulfilling ones, they need, while at school and university, to be able to acquire the knowledge and skills that will enable them to get jobs that they believe are socially useful and that will make full use of their abilities, and also to have access to good careers and labour market information. This is not what happens today. And the fact that currently there are many vacancies for technicians at a time when there are many young unemployed people who have the ability to fill them must be seen as a major failure of our education and training system. If we want to produce more 'good quality' jobs – that is, jobs with hours and pay that lift families out of poverty, and provide opportunities for training and promotion – then this is a policy failure that we must tackle.

It is also a failure that has serious economic consequences. In its 2010 National Strategic Skills Audit, the UK Commission for Employment and Skills highlighted an urgent need for technicians within sectors of high economic importance: manufacturing, oil, gas, electricity, chemicals, pharmaceuticals, automotive, engineering and broadcasting. And in the Organisation for Economic Co-operation and Development's comparisons of 30 countries, the UK scores 11th on 'high' but only 20th on 'intermediate skills'. Many studies over the years have shown the harmful effect this lack of technician skills has on UK productivity.

This lack of good technicians has been a major problem for the economy for over 100 years, during which time there have been many well-meaning attempts to improve it, though without success. To make progress in improving the supply of technicians, we first need to agree what are the key institutional features of an effective system of technician education and training. These are a well-understood national system of qualifications for transferable technician skills that works in the marketplace, a system of funding young people while they acquire the qualifications, and the teachers and facilities to train the young people.

A well-understood national system of qualification that works in the marketplace is required because young people will not undertake a rigorous course of study unless they know that the qualifications that they acquire at the end of it, if they are successful, will mean that they can get a job with better pay and security. Also, most young people do not have the resources to pay for a lengthy course of study, and obviously, if there are no good teachers or facilities available, they cannot acquire the necessary skills. These three key institutional features of an effective system of technician education and training exist in Germany, which has an excellent system of technician training and education, but are largely absent in the UK.

It will be argued by some people that the increase in the number of apprenticeships over recent years means that this is a problem which is well on the way to being solved. But it is important to understand what the figures show. Of the 500,000 apprenticeship starts in 2012/2013, some 300,000 were intermediate apprenticeships at level 2, which means they are not being trained to a technician level of qualification. And of the roughly 200,000 taking advanced apprenticeships at level 3, only some 42,000 were in science, engineering and technology areas, which is where there are the major problems. In fairness it should be said that if we did produce 40,000 well-educated and trained technicians in these areas each year for the next 10 years, it would go some way to solving our shortage of key technicians. But the assessment procedures for all apprenticeships are very poor, and the apprenticeship system does not give young people a national qualification that works in the marketplace.

That is why we should set up of a new system of technician education and training that is based on using the professional institutions that cover the scientific, medical, IT and engineering areas. The professional bodies have high prestige in the UK, they all have national qualification systems that work in the marketplace, and in a few cases they already have a registered technician qualification. The basic idea of the new system is that all apprenticeships supported with government money should cover the technical knowledge required to become a registered technician, so that if an apprentice passes an effective assessment, he or she can, after possibly gaining some more practical experience, automatically become a registered technician. In this way they will acquire a national qualification that works in the marketplace.

The professional bodies are now embracing this idea. Where they do not have registered technician qualifications they are designing them, and where they do have them they are looking at promoting them more strongly. It is also very encouraging that the government has now said that all the new technical trailblazer apprenticeships should be aligned with the relevant professional technician qualifications.

If, however, the Registered Technician Scheme is going to have a major impact, it will need the government to support it by reforming further education colleges. This is an area that has long been neglected by governments. As a result, the colleges do not have a clear mission, providing as they do a mixture of remedial education, adult education and technician-level knowledge and training. Their funding system also has a number of flaws. Because it is done on an annual cycle, colleges face an increased challenge in planning their curriculum offer. Furthermore, teaching staff are often on short-term contracts, which does not make for a high standard of teaching. The colleges are also poorly equipped, and the funding does not ensure that the colleges are closely linked to local industry needs, which is essential for this type of education and training.

In all these areas government needs to make changes if it wants to provide more opportunities for young people who are not going to university to get skilled jobs. It should make clear that the central mission of colleges is to provide young people with technician-level knowledge and skills. It should put the funding on a triennial basis, it should provide funds so that the colleges are properly equipped, and it should make the funding of colleges dependent on them providing plans closely linked to the needs of local industry.

Finally, the setting-up of University Technical Colleges by the Baker Dearing Trust has the potential to play a major role in the education and training of technicians by remedying one of the most serious failures of the UK's educational system, the failure to have a technical pathway in our schools. Seventy years ago the visionary 1944 Education Act proposed that technical schools should be part of a tripartite system. But neglect, academic snobbery and the absurdity of selecting children for the three streams on the basis of a test administered at the age of 11 meant, disastrously, that a technical pathway never became part of our school system. The University Technical Colleges present an opportunity to correct that terrible mistake.

The reform of the UK's education and training system for technicians is vitally important both for dealing with the problem of youth unemployment and raising the rate of economic growth in this country, and if we want to create a more equal society and a more dynamic economy, it should be put high up on the political agenda.

FURTHER DISCUSSION OF WHAT NEEDS TO BE DONE

The UK's workforce is more qualified now than it has ever been, but employers still say that a shortage of people with the right skills is the biggest impediment to growth. Getting skills policy – and vocational education and training in particular – right would play a big part in closing the productivity gap between the UK and countries like Germany and France. It would also help to reduce youth unemployment and smooth the transition from education to meaningful work.

Reforming Vocational Education and Training

As a first step, the architecture of the vocational education and training framework needs to be rethought. It is impossible for central government and its agencies to judge local skills needs. While it is important that there is national leadership over the standards required to achieve qualifications, entitlements to education and training and any accompanying financial support and funding, other responsibilities should be devolved to sectoral or industrial partnership structures and to city regions or local authorities. This could include the mix of training provided and details of curricula.

A primary function of the education system, and the vocational education and training system in particular, should be to increase the employability and potential productivity of young people in the UK. This means that from around the age of 14, and particularly after the age of 16, teaching and training should begin to have more regard for what young people will do after completing their education. This does not necessarily mean every young person is being trained for a particular career from the age of 14 – far from it. But it does mean they should be beginning to learn skills they will need in the workplace, including problem solving, team work and oral communication, for example.

If the UK's vocational education and training system is judged by its ability to deliver the right mix of skills to the economy, then it is clearly not working well. The UK has severe skill shortages in key technician level jobs. Yet, at the same time, there are many graduates who are working in jobs that do not require someone with a degree to do them; there are many employers who are underutilising the skills that their employees possess; and the UK has a higher proportion of low-skilled jobs in its workforce than other comparable countries and a relatively high rate of youth unemployment.

The problem is not, therefore, a simple shortage of skills, but rather a skills mismatch combined with a low-skilled equilibrium. This has enormous negative consequences for the performance of the UK economy. Productivity in the UK is around a fifth lower than in Germany and France. A failure to develop and fully utilise the skills of our young people over many years has contributed to the opening up of this gap. Unless our vocational education and training system is reformed, it will not be possible to close it.

Too often in the UK, vocational education and training is represented as a lesser alternative to higher education – picking up the slack of those who are not expected to achieve the A-level results needed to go to university. It should instead be seen as a pathway into high-skilled work in its own right, with just as much status as the university route (as it is in, for example, Germany and Austria). For some students, following the vocational route should mean going on to study for a degree or for advanced qualifications that are equivalent to a degree.

The aim should be for almost all young people who do not take the university route to study for, and achieve, a level 3 qualification, with a significant proportion going on to study at a higher level with greater specialisation. For the most part, it is only at level 3 that qualifications combine general educational skills with some vocational specialisation and an element of work experience. For this reason those with level 3 qualifications earn a significant wage premium over those without them, suggesting this is the crucial level in terms of delivering higher productivity in the workplace.

At 16, those choosing not to study A-levels should, if they have a level 2 qualification, be entitled to a choice between a level 3 apprenticeship or a place on a level 3 full-time vocational course with guaranteed work-based training. Those without a level 2 qualification should be entitled to education and training to help them achieve this level, with an emphasis on literacy, numeracy and IT skills (possibly through 'applied GCSEs'), though the ultimate aim should be to reduce the numbers in this group. Currently, too much further education provision in the UK has to be devoted to bringing young people aged 17 and 18 up to level 2 in key subjects, particularly mathematics and English. This uses up valuable resources and leaves them without the time to gain a level 3 qualification before their free education ends.

To encourage young people to acquire more skills, a youth allowance should be introduced. This would be available equally to young people in education and training (even if they were not actively looking for work) and to those who are not in education or training but are actively seeking employment. It would encourage young people to continue their education and acquire the skills that employers are looking for. The allowance could be paid at the same rate as Jobseekers' Allowance for those aged under 25 years old (currently £57.35 a week).

Ensuring High Standards for Vocational Education and Training Qualifications

A well-understood national system of qualifications is a prerequisite for a well-functioning vocational education and training system. Without such a system, employers cannot easily identify the level of knowledge and skills acquired by job applicants and young people cannot know how useful the qualifications they might consider studying for will be in the labour market. The UK's system is not well understood by young people or potential employers, not least because of the bewildering and incoherent array of options it presents. A single set of vocational qualifications should be designated for all 16- to 19-year-old students. It is important, though, that there is consistency of standards across the country and across different subjects. At present, the relationship between qualifications and skills is weak and this makes it hard for employers to judge potential employees. Oversight is needed to ensure that the attainment of a level 3 qualification is only possible if an agreed level of skills is acquired.

Many vocational qualifications in the UK are not recognised by employers. In Germany, this is not a problem because trade associations play a large part in setting the standards for vocational qualifications, including apprenticeships. Their UK equivalents – the sector skills councils – have not demonstrated the capacity to fulfil a similar role, and experience suggests attempts to make them more like the German associations would fail because importing institutional ideas from one country to another rarely succeeds. Instead, the UK should make use of existing institutions where they exist. For example, professional institutions in fields such as science, engineering, IT and healthcare should be encouraged to specify the level of knowledge and skills required to become a 'registered technician' in these fields. Apprentices who reached the required levels in an assessed demonstration of their abilities and who had sufficient work experience would qualify to become such a registered technician.

Apprenticeships should be a central element in ensuring that the UK's vocational education and training system produces the number of technicians that the country needs, but this is not currently the case. Apprenticeships are held in low esteem by young people in the UK, rather than being seen as a high-quality vocational route into the workforce. Variable standards mean that their worth is hard to judge for both students and potential employers.

There has been a massive increase in the number of apprenticeships in recent years but not in a way that means more young people are being trained to fill the technician vacancies in the economy. Most of the increase has been accounted for by people aged 25 and over; young people aged 16 to 24 now account for less than three in five apprenticeships. Only two in five apprenticeships are at level 3, and only one in five of these are in the areas of science, engineering and technology. There has been a proliferation of low-level training for existing employees in areas such as retailing, customer service and hospitality and catering masquerading as apprenticeships, while the number of young people achieving high-level apprenticeships in engineering has not increased.

A number of steps are required to reclaim the apprenticeship brand so that it is associated with a high-quality route into work for young people. These include only letting people aged 23 and under start an apprenticeship (other than in exceptional cases); restricting apprenticeships to be level 3 and above and requiring them to last for at least a year; and requiring at least 30 per cent of an apprentice's time to be spent in off-the-job training.

However, the solution to the UK's skills problem is not to develop a world-class apprenticeship system with a second-rate full-time vocational education and training system alongside it. Full-time vocational education and training should lead to a qualification that is as highly regarded by employers as a successfully completed apprenticeship. Full-time study should mean 30 hours a week, not 15 hours as at present, and should include at least 10 weeks of work experience in a year. Every full-time course should involve on-the-job experience, preferably with a number of employers. This will help students decide between different potential work options, allow both students and employers to assess each other before any future job offer is made or accepted and, most crucially, give students the work experience that employers say is vital in new recruits.

In theory, it should be easier to engage small and medium-sized businesses with vocational education and training rather than apprenticeships because they do not have the capacity to take on apprentices. However, one hindrance to improving vocational education and training in practice is likely to be the shortage of practical work-based experience offered by employers. A lack of employer engagement means colleges often have to create work experience opportunities (for example, having IT students work on the college helpdesk). Such simulated opportunities are a poor, second-best alternative to work experience with external employers and more needs to be done to encourage local firms to offer work placements to students.

Involving Employers

Employers need to be more involved in vocational education and training, but the presumption has grown in the UK that the provision of skills is something that the state does, with minimal input from employers. At the same time, variable standards in further education have led to disillusionment with the training system. A new strategy is needed to engage more employers, particularly among small and medium-sized firms, who struggle to understand the benefits of workforce development and who in many cases did not themselves participate in good-quality vocational education and training. This means providing employers with access to high-quality business support to help them improve their businesses by creating jobs and workplaces that are more highly skilled. The types of providers that receive public funds for vocational education and training should be consolidated into a network of high-quality institutions that is capable of providing business support as part of a holistic service for employers.

None of these changes will be effective if the focus and quality of further education is not improved. For too long further education has been the 'poor relation' of the education system: under-resourced relative to the rest of the system, meaning that it cannot attract the best teachers and offer first-class training facilities. The result is patchy provision: excellent in some subjects and in some parts of the country, but not in others. This random spread of excellence makes it hard for young people to choose the right courses and hard for employers to assess the quality of education and training that a job applicant has received. Where provision is not good, it also represents an under-utilisation of resources.

Improving vocational education and training will require a national system of qualifications that works in the market place and better teaching and facilities in colleges. The government needs to find additional resources for colleges; get rid of agencies that have ill-defined responsibilities for vocational education and training (and that tend to regard the achievement of more and more qualifications as a successful outcome); and ensure that awarding bodies are not a barrier to greater employer involvement. The government should also make additional resources available to allow colleges to update their facilities and to attract better teachers, trained as specialist vocational teachers and trainers. Funding should be provided on at least a three-year basis to allow colleges to plan better and to offer longer contracts to staff. In return, colleges would have to make delivering 'employability' their central focus, rather than delivering qualifications, and they would have to publish details not just of the qualifications achieved by their students, but also their destinations upon leaving college. This shift of focus would require colleges to offer more courses that deliver the qualifications demanded by local employers, and fewer of those that do not. Ultimately, one effect of this shift of focus should be to increase the number of people trained to be technicians.

Expanding University Technical Colleges and Careers Colleges

University Technical Colleges, which take young people from the age of 14 to 18, can be a more direct route to achieving the same aim by filling a long-standing gap in the UK's education system: the lack of a technical pathway in schools. They offer a rounded education, including mathematics, English and science, but they also require students to spend 40 per cent of their time following a technical specialism. They have close links with local universities and employers to ensure that the curriculum in their technical specialisms is up-to-date and relevant to the local labour market. The aim is that at 16 young people in UTCs will be in a position to start a level 3 vocational qualification, including an apprenticeship, giving them time to go on and achieve level 3 and level 4 qualifications before they take up full-time work.

UTCs are potentially a major positive innovation in the UK's education system and it is planned that by 2016 more than 30,000 students will be studying in them. However, this represents only a very small proportion of the 14 to 18 age group and the choice of specialism for any individual student is limited at present. Each UTC specialises in only one or two technical areas and they are dispersed around the country so only one or two will be realistic options. More are needed to make a real difference to vocational education and training in the UK.

Improving the vocational skills of the young people entering the UK's workforce is not all about skills in science and technology; there are skills gaps in other areas. Careers Colleges are being developed to complement UTCs. While UTCs will provide vocational training in science, technology and engineering, Careers Colleges will focus on non-Stem (science, technology engineering and mathematics) subjects. Like UTCs, Careers Colleges will also take advantage of the decision to allow further education colleges to recruit children at the age of 14 and will provide teaching in the core curriculum subjects, including English, mathematics and science, but in the context of a chosen vocational specialism. They will also provide vocational learning, including hands-on projects, which will be facilitated by getting local employers involved in the design and delivery of the curriculum.

Like any new institution, UTCs and Careers Colleges are probably regarded with a degree of suspicion by young people and their parents. Understandably, their very newness creates a barrier to 14-year-olds making a decision to leave their school to join them and enrolment rates are reported to have been disappointing. But it might also be that there are genuine worries about the degree of specialisation at 14 (even allowing for the fact that mathematics and

English are taught at least to GCSE level). If these worries can be met, perhaps by reducing the degree of specialisation from age 14 to 16, and if over time UTCs gain a positive reputation for delivering good outcomes for their students, they have the potential to become a central part of the country's vocational learning pathway.

Overhauling Careers Advice and Guidance

The development of University Technical Colleges and Careers Colleges and the option for further education colleges to take on students from the age of 14 has opened up the question of what decisions young people should be making about their studies at what age. Traditionally in the UK, the key choices have been at age 11 – the transfer from primary to secondary education – and at 16 – whether to study for A-levels or a different qualification, or to enter the workforce (or to opt for some combination). At the age of 14 there was the important, but less significant, choice to make of GSCE subjects (or alternatives). Almost by accident, it seems, the UK is moving to a system in which young people have to make a more crucial choice at 14 of where and what to study. There is a good case for formalising this shift – for example, by applying the national curriculum only up to the age of 14, while at the same time ensuring that young people who find themselves on the wrong pathway are able to make a change. Age 11 is too early for young people to choose a pathway, but age 16 is too late to allow young people time to progress to level 3 vocational qualifications before their free education runs out.

Increasing choice for young people at the age of 14 creates an obligation to provide additional support for them in the form of high-quality careers education and advice. Once it is accepted that a primary function of the education system is to give young people the knowledge and skills they need to get jobs, then it is clear that more attention should be given to the amount and quality of careers education and guidance in schools and colleges. At the moment young people have many options to choose from and are given too little advice to help them make the right choice. Poor careers advice and guidance contributes to young people entering the labour market with the wrong qualifications and skills for the jobs that are available.

Careers education and guidance and the provision of information about the local labour market are crucial in ensuring a smooth transition from education to work in European countries with low rates of youth unemployment, but they have never been seen as important in the UK. Careers education can help young people understand the nature of work; tell them about the different types of jobs that can be found in a modern economy; and describe what skills are required for any particular career. Careers guidance, when combined with good information about the local labour market, can help young people make the right choices about education and training so that they can embark on a career that suits their interests and aptitudes.

There should not be strict rules about the amount of in-house or bought-in careers education and guidance that is provided, but every secondary school should be required to appoint a full-time careers officer or director of enterprise and employment. This person would be an expert in the local labour market, rather than someone with teaching experience, and responsible for careers education and guidance and for getting local employers more involved in schools. They should provide students with up-to-date information on education and training options and on opportunities in the local labour market and coordinate the provision of careers guidance, which should be carried out by specialist advisers.

The quantity and quality of careers education and guidance should be a prime consideration for parents and students when they are choosing secondary schools. The work of the careers officer should be published in schools' reports. All schools should be required to set out clearly, on their websites and in their prospectuses, their plans for careers education and guidance. Ideally, this should be done alongside data showing the destinations of students leaving the school. The same requirement should be placed on further education colleges that take in students at the age of 14, including University Technical Colleges and Careers Colleges.

Inevitably, though, there is a limit to what can be achieved by careers advice, and even a dedicated careers officer would find it hard to remain abreast of all developments in the local jobs market. Their knowledge is also likely to be general in nature. This is why work experience is so important. Young people can learn more about a job in a few days than they could ever pick up from careers advice interviews.

There would also seem to be a role for 'big-data' analysis here. There is a huge amount of information on pathways, qualifications, wages and job vacancies available on the internet from a range of sources, much of it with a geographical tag. Someone needs to be incentivised to bring it all together in a way that is useful and easily accessible by young people.

CONCLUSION

Vocational education and training is a much smaller part of the UK's education system than is the case in many other European countries. This contributes to the gap between average productivity levels in the UK and these countries. The UK's vocational education and training system needs to be overhauled to make it central to economic growth and productivity advances. This could take up to a decade and will require cross-party support.

Continuous change to the education and training system in the past has been cited as a major reason for its current failings, leading to calls for stability. But the system is clearly not working to facilitate a smooth transition from education to meaningful employment for many young people. Stability will lock in this failure. The vocational education and training system must be reformed so that it is better designed to give young people the skills they need to thrive in the workforce. The problem with change in the past is that it has been piecemeal. Another round of change can be justified, if it involves fundamental change leading to a truly superior system.

REFORMING CORPORATE GOVERNANCE TO ENCOURAGE LONG-TERM THINKING AND INVESTMENT

THE CASE FOR REFORM AND THE DIRECTION IT SHOULD TAKE

If we stand back and look at how the relationship between shareholders and firms has developed over the last 50 years in the UK, it is clear that it has worsened rather than improved. This is because changes in the equity markets have led many investment managers to adopt short-term investment strategies. As a result, they have no interest in exercising their rights as shareholders, and we have 'capitalism without owners'. This is a flawed system given that a defining characteristic of capitalism is the holding of the productive assets of a country by individuals who have a direct interest in making certain they are used efficiently over the long term.

At the same time, the widespread use of a deeply flawed version of financial-markets-based compensation has led not only to a large and extremely damaging financial incentive bubble but also to executives often adopting very short-term strategies for their companies. For example, it makes perfect sense in today's circumstances for an executive whose bonuses depend on his company's short-term return on equity or earnings per share to use the company's spare cash to buy back shares rather than invest for the long term. This is one of the factors which may have been holding back investment in this country in recent years.

A long series of corporate codes of conduct have been introduced to try to remedy the problems arising from the providers of capital and investment managers not exercising their rights as owners, starting with the Cadbury Code in 1992. This contained two main provisions: that the chairman's role should in principle be separate from that of the chief executive, and that a majority of the board ought to be non-executive directors. While the Cadbury Code and those that followed it have formalised numerous key board processes, and made it more difficult for the chief executive of a company to run it to further personal interests, it is doubtful whether they have done much to improve the governance of UK companies, as the lack of control over executive salaries shows.

The continuing failure of investment managers to get involved in the governance of the companies in which they invest has meant that non-executive directors of companies have been effectively appointed by the management of those companies and have not, therefore, been prepared to stand up to them when they believe that the company is not being managed as it should be. The emphasis of the codes of conduct has largely been on preventing the destruction of wealth rather than on its long-term creation, and they have been the cause, not surprisingly, of a considerable amount of pointless box-ticking.

What should be done to reform the governance of UK companies so that the incentives for executives are aligned with the long-term interests of their companies and do not lead to damaging financial incentive bubbles?

First, the government should mobilise the various bodies that represent shareholders to form a new Shareholders Advisory Board to advise all shareholders on how to contract and deal with investment managers. Specifically, they should encourage all the bodies which hold the assets of savers to fundamentally alter the way they contract and deal with investment managers. In the future the emphasis should be on investment based on an understanding of the fundamental value of the companies in which they invest, rather than on 'trading' based on the likely short-term movements of share prices. The new Shareholders Advisory Board should also encourage all the bodies which hold the assets of savers to review the performance of investment managers at intervals no less than every three to five years, and with reference to long-term absolute performance.

Second, the Shareholders Advisory Board should facilitate and promote the use of nomination committees based on the model used in Sweden. In both the UK and Sweden, nomination committees are the body with responsibility for finding the right people to serve on boards. In the UK, however, the nomination committee is a subcommittee of the board. It is made up of board members and is usually chaired by the chair of the board. Board candidates are proposed by the nomination committee to the Annual General Meeting (AGM) and in the normal course of events are elected. In Sweden, on the other hand, the nomination committee is a servant of the AGM. It is not made up of board members, but mainly of four or five of the largest owners of shares in the company. It has its mandate from the shareholders at the AGM. It recommends to the shareholders at the AGM who should join the board, which is primarily made up of non-executives, as well as the structure and amount of remuneration of each director, and procedural issues for the appointment of the following year's nomination committee. The remuneration of executive management is handled separately by the board. As a result, non-executives feel that their first loyalty is to the shareholders, and are much more prepared to stand up to the executive directors.

Third, in order to improve both the functions of equity markets and corporate governance in the UK, takeovers should be made more difficult. They should not be stopped entirely, because there are occasions when putting two businesses together creates real synergy and added value. But there is a substantial body of academic evidence that suggests that little or no value is added to businesses by most merger activity. The threat of a takeover, and the frequent reporting of performance, results in managers taking a short-term view and underinvesting in physical assets or intangibles such as product development, employee skills and reputation with customers. Two simple changes should be made: the level of acceptances required from shareholders in the target company should be raised and voting in the target company should be restricted to those who have held shares for more than a certain number of years.

Fourth, the government should work with the Shareholder Advisory Board to draw up a code for executive remuneration which aligns it more closely to the long-term performance of executives' companies, does not lead to an unjustified escalation of executive remuneration and cannot be so easily manipulated.

There will no doubt be those who will argue that these reforms would be in conflict with a free market. But if you look at them closely, you will see that they are designed both to make capitalism work as it is supposed to work and to stop people exploiting the system. These reforms should, therefore, be supported by all progressive politicians.

FURTHER DISCUSSION OF WHAT NEEDS TO BE DONE

If the UK economy is to grow in a more balanced way in the future and compete in global markets, it needs to have a higher rate of business investment in innovation and productive capacity. The UK regularly comes near the bottom of international league tables for investment and its ratio of investment to gross domestic product has been persistently below that in the other G7 economies. A major reason for the UK's low rate of investment is the short-term strategies adopted by companies. Implementing major investment projects requires companies to take a long-term view: gauging the future evolution of demand for their products and the cost of inputs, taking into account the risks and uncertainties, and being prepared to devote resources to investment projects. Firms in the UK have preferred to focus on the short term. This is the result of the way that the shareholder corporate model has developed in the UK: in particular, the approach of investment managers and how executives are remunerated.

Countering the Short-Term Thinking of Managements and Company Boards

The investment management industry has become more focused on the short term. Managers are required to report quarterly performance figures to their clients and receive performance fees that are often determined by annual returns. Fund managers are also, therefore, more interested in the next set of results that a company will produce than in its long-term prospects. Receiving this message from the representatives of their shareholders, corporate management has reacted accordingly, focusing on short-term performance and embedding this in companies' incentive schemes. The result is an unwillingness to take a long-term view and invest in research, product development, new productive capacity and staff training. Another is executive pay schemes that are linked to short-term growth or profits, because these are seen to be what shareholders are most concerned about.

Starting in the financial sector but spreading across much of the rest of the economy, the structure of executive compensation packages in the UK has moved in a direction that encourages short-term thinking. Executives whose bonuses depend on the next set of quarterly financial reports try to ensure that they are as strong as possible. In particular, giving them leveraged options on their company's share price as a large part of their remuneration has created a huge incentive for senior managers to push up their company's earnings per share or return on equity in the short term, even if this does not represent the best long-term strategy for the company. Similarly, they are more likely to use spare cash to buy back the company's shares than for long-term investment projects.

The adoption of short-term investment strategies by investment managers has also changed their relationship with the firms they invest in. Whereas 30 or 40 years ago, investment managers bought shares with a view to holding them for a number of years and so tried to acquire a good understanding of companies' medium to long-term business strategies, this is no longer deemed necessary. Shares are held for much shorter periods: in the hope that the next few quarterly reports will beat expectations or that a company will become a potential takeover target. Investment managers feel much less need to engage with management over the long-term prospects of a company. They have become traders of shares rather than owners of companies and they are far less interested in exercising their rights as shareholders. The result is the disappearance of the old idea of share ownership and the transition to a system with weak owners and strong managers, what some have called 'capitalism without owners'.

This gives enormous power to the senior management of companies, who are able to operate with far fewer constraints. Despite a series of codes of conduct, reports and reviews, all designed to make it harder for senior executives of a company to run it in their own interests, company chairmen and non-executive directors are still drawn from a small pool of men and an even smaller pool of women, who are well-known to senior executives. Too often, non-executive directors – and even chairmen – are effectively appointed by the senior management of companies and therefore lack the independence needed to question their judgement.

This failure is well illustrated by the extraordinary growth in the pay of senior executives in the last 20 to 30 years. Not only have company boards signed off massive increases in salaries, they have also acquiesced to the creation of short-term bonus schemes and the use of share options to reward senior management. These were supposed to align the interests of managers with those of shareholders, but they have resulted in huge increases in management remuneration during a period when the returns to shareholders have been modest. They have also encouraged short-term thinking, ironically in no small part due to increased transparency in company reporting.

The desire of every company to ensure that its senior management team is paid in line with, or even a little above, the average has led to a ratcheting up of pay. Company boards, which should be primarily concerned with the long-term health and growth of their companies, have instead allowed companies to be managed for the short-term gain of their senior managers.

If the UK economy is to be transformed through a higher rate of investment, there will have to be big changes to the governance of companies. Senior executives have to be encouraged to focus more on the long-term interests of their companies and less on short-term performance. This will not happen as a result of exhortation – people in the system are not behaving irrationally or, in their own eyes, immorally. The issues are structural or systemic in nature. Government – in consultation with all the relevant stakeholders – has to tackle the issues and use the appropriate mix of taxation, regulation, quasi-regulation (such as enforced codes of behaviour) and self-regulation to bring about change to incentive packages and other practices. Some of the necessary changes might be brought about within the existing shareholder model, but the obstacles are formidable and a greater involvement of long-term shareholders is needed.

Making Shareholders More Effective Stewards of Firms

The UK's system of corporate governance emphasises the role of shareholders in influencing senior management, directly and through company boards, to improve company performance. In practice, this approach has been revealed to have a number of weaknesses. It takes no account of other stakeholders in the company: shareholders are incentivised to pursue their own interests, even to the detriment of these other stakeholders, including employees, customers and suppliers. But shareholders have not been very effective at pursuing even their own interests, leaving executives to manage companies largely in their own interests.

If the shareholder model is to be made to function better, investment managers will have to engage more with companies about their long-term prospects, but this will only happen if their clients require them to do so. Large investors, such as pension funds, should be encouraged to hire managers that invest on the basis of the fundamental long-term value of the companies in which they invest. This will require greater patience on their part. Rather than judging – and rewarding – their investment managers on the basis of annual performance, they should commit to longer contracts of at least three years, and preferably even longer. Performance should be judged over this longer period and any performance fee should be based on long-term returns.

This will not be an easy change to bring about: investors are very conservative by nature and will be reluctant to be in the vanguard of a move to do things differently; investment managers are happy with the current situation, which allows them to charge high fees for short-term outperformance without any downside when they underperform; and there is a whole industry of advisers who survive by recommending frequent switches of investment strategies and managers. It may need a new type of investment management company to emerge. The government will therefore have to play a part, in conjunction with bodies that represent investors, such as the National Association of Pension Funds. It should establish a body to influence the requirements investors place on their managers and specifically to push the case for managers who invest on the basis of long-term value.

Investment managers also need to be encouraged to take a greater interest – on behalf of their clients, the ultimate shareholders – in the companies in which they invest. This should start with the composition of the board. In the UK, new non-executive board members are typically appointed on the recommendation of a nomination committee made up of the chairman and existing board members, including executives. Although appointments have to be confirmed at an AGM, this is usually a formality. This procedure is a recipe for producing boards that are unlikely to challenge the judgement of the chairman and chief executive, and have little sense of responsibility to shareholders.

If the first loyalty of non-executive board members should be to shareholders, then they should be appointed by a nomination committee that is made up entirely, or mainly, of shareholders appointed by the AGM. Normally, this would comprise a small number of the largest owners of shares, as represented by investment managers. Moving to this model would ensure that non-executive board members are more independent of the company management. When selecting these members, shareholders, or their representatives, would have to trade-off independence and knowledge of the industry in which the company operates. Someone who has been in an industry for many years would be a useful member of the board because of the knowledge and experience they could bring to it. But, by virtue of having been in the industry for so long, they are likely to know the executives of the firm and thus less likely to be seen as independent. On the other hand, a genuinely independent board member is likely to come from a different part of the economy and, while they might still bring useful skills and experience to the board, may not be best placed to make strategic decisions about the company's future direction.

A move to more independent non-executive board members should bring with it a change in remuneration packages for senior executives so that they are more aligned with the long-term interests of the company and shareholders. Bonuses should be paid in shares in the company and only vest after a suitably long period of time – at least the length of a normal economic cycle – say, seven years.

Again, change will have to be driven through by the ultimate shareholders. At present, investment managers are part of the problem. They can earn far more than the company directors they are supposed to be overseeing, not least because their own non-executive board members have allowed massive increases in remuneration for senior executives and a shortening of time horizons. It is hard to envisage them voluntarily becoming part of the solution. The government should draw up a code for executive remuneration that aligns it more closely to the long-term performance of executives and their companies. Investors should then require their investment managers, when they form part of a nomination committee, only to select non-executive directors who agree to implement this code.

The fragmentation of share ownership means that these reforms rely heavily on large domestic investors, who own only a fraction of UK shares, pulling well above their weight. Although some overseas investors in UK shares, such as sovereign wealth funds, might also have an interest in good corporate governance, other investors with very small stakes are unlikely to become involved, preferring instead to free ride on the back of the efforts of others.

Developing a Stakeholder Approach to Company Management

The inherent obstacles that face any attempt to make the shareholder model work better means that other changes need to occur too. In particular, companies should be incentivised, or required, to adopt a more stakeholder model. Rather than seeking to maximise shareholder value alone, executives would manage their companies in a way that balanced the interests of employees, customers and suppliers, as well as shareholders.

One suggestion designed to move companies in this direction is the idea that company boards should be more diverse and contain representatives from all stakeholders. This might take the form of a continental-style supervisory board made up of non-executives that operates in conjunction with a separate executive management board. Or it could more simply mean retaining a single board but making changes to its composition. If a board contained a representative of the company's workforce, for example, this might act as a constraint on behaviour, particularly in matters of senior management pay.

The problem with this proposal, as it is usually set out, is that it sets up the workers' representative as a delegate to the board, representing a particular constituency's interests. This is not how boards are supposed to work; they should be there to represent the interests of the whole company and its stakeholders, including the shareholders. It is also no guarantee of greater long-term thinking. A company's workforce – and thus its representative – is likely to prioritise higher pay and avoiding the loss of jobs, which at times might be in conflict with the need for greater spending on innovation or investment.

This does not mean that the idea of the workforce – or other stakeholders – being represented on the board is a bad one; their knowledge of the business could help to inform the company's future direction. But it only works if the aims of the representatives are aligned with those of other board members, and ultimately if they are all working in the long-term interests of the company.

There are alternative ways of ensuring that the workers' views are taken into account. Elected councils, alongside increased employee ownership and the participation of all employees in profit-sharing schemes, can give workers a real voice in the running of a company – and the incentive to participate – if senior management are prepared to listen. They would be foolish not to. Research has shown that companies in which employees have a stake and a say tend to be more productive.

Making Takeovers Harder to Complete

The risk of becoming a takeover target can also cause managers of companies to focus excessively on their short-term results, to the detriment of long-term investment in innovation, additional capacity and the skills of their workers. Yet most mergers and acquisitions do not create additional value. It would be wrong to ban takeovers entirely, but there is a good case for making them more difficult.

Policy can discourage takeovers in two simple ways. First, a greater proportion of shareholders should be required to vote in favour of a takeover before it can go ahead. Second, there should be restrictions on which shareholders of a company can vote on a proposed takeover. When a company announces its intention to bid for another company, it is quite common for short-term investors such as hedge funds to buy shares in the target company with the intention of holding out for a higher bid and then forcing through a sale. It is wrong that the long-term future of companies can be determined by short-term speculators in this way. Only those who have held shares in a company for a certain period – perhaps one year – at the time of a bid should be allowed to vote on any proposed takeover of the company.

This change could be backed up by incentives to encourage long-term shareholding. Abolishing the quarterly reporting of companies' results and moving to six-monthly, or even annual, reporting, might have some effect on approaches to investing, but changes in tax offer more promise. If the tax treatment of equity and debt was equalised (for example, through the introduction of an allowance for corporate equity), issuing and holding shares would be more attractive. Tapering capital gains tax, so that it is applied at a very high rate for short-term gains (over less than a year), falling to a very low rate, or even zero, for long-term gains (over ten years), would encourage investors to hold onto shares for longer.

CONCLUSION

Better corporate governance in the UK would contribute to a rebalancing of the economy, through higher investment, and increase its long-term stability. It is therefore a prize worth aiming for. Given the dominance of the shareholder model of capitalism in the UK, many proposals for improving governance centre around the shareholder, and the need to get the ultimate owners of equities to force their investment managers to adopt new practices and for them in turn to force change on companies. There are some obvious obstacles to this approach. Investment managers are happy with the status quo; they do not want to be responsible for the long-term health of companies or the economy, and push back against attempts to make them change. Senior managers in companies are also happy with the high remuneration they receive under the current way of doing things.

It is easy to see what is needed: to align the interests of management with the long-term performance of their companies and of the economy as a whole so as to encourage greater investment in research, product development, physical capacity and the skills of their workforces. Bonuses that depend more on the growth of investment and output over the long term, rather than profits in the short term, would be easy to design, but it is much harder to see how companies can be persuaded to introduce them. Exhortation alone is unlikely to be sufficient. The government will have to drive through change, working with large investors, to shift incentives and force changes in behaviour using tax, regulation and codes of practice.

DEVELOPING A FINANCIAL SYSTEM THAT MEETS THE NEEDS OF THE REST OF THE ECONOMY

THE CASE FOR REFORM AND THE DIRECTION IT SHOULD TAKE

Finance is an essential part of any modern economy. A well-functioning financial system is needed to intermediate between lenders and borrowers, evaluate business proposals, manage people's assets, help companies raise funds, direct resources to where returns are likely to be highest and facilitate the trading of financial assets. These roles should be performed without charging excessive fees and without creating financial crises. The financial crash of 2008 is the most obvious among many signs that the UK's system is not working and needs to be reformed.

If one is going to reform a country's institutions, it will be necessary both to understand how its institutions work and to come up with credible new institutions which will work better. This is not easy to do, which is perhaps why we have not seen from either the coalition government or the Labour party a coherent narrative about what caused the financial crash of 2008 or why our financial institutions need to be reformed so that they perform their function better.

While most economists are still in denial about the financial crash of 2008, because according to neoclassical economics it should never have happened, the explanation for it is fairly simple. A key cause of the financial crash was the decision by Alan Greenspan and the Federal Reserve to keep the funds rate below 2.5 per cent from November 2001 to February 2005. The result was a borrowing binge by homeowners, consumers, businesses and speculators, and a massive housing bubble, which burst in mid-2007.

Such bubbles, and the disasters they bring, are, of course, as old as capitalism and banking itself. What made it so lethal this time was four major institutional failures, all of which can be attributed to the lack of effective regulation: the uncontrolled growth of subprime mortgages and their securitisation; the high level of debt taken on by the banks; the lack of transparency of bank balance sheets and the use of 'special-purpose vehicles'; and the uncontrolled growth of derivatives. Each of these institutional failures had disastrous consequences, and a great deal more thought should be given as to whether sufficient reforms have been made so that these failures will not happen again.

It is also the case that in the years leading up to the financial crash of 2008, the UK's equity markets did not perform effectively the essential function that society requires them to perform. The long-term purpose of financial markets is to allocate capital to high-performing companies, on the basis of low transaction costs, and thereby provide savers with high returns. They have clearly not done this in recent years. It is also important to understand that UK equity markets are no longer a significant source of funding for new investment by UK companies. Large UK companies are self-financing: the cash flow generated by their operations being more than they need for investment. The relatively small number of UK companies which access the new issue market often use it as a means of achieving liquidity for early-stage investors, rather than to raise funds for new investment.

In this context, competition between asset managers on the basis of relative performance is inherently a zero-sum game: if one investment manager does particularly well, it will be at the expense of another one doing particularly badly. In such a situation the asset management industry can benefit its customers – its savers taken as a whole – only to the extent that its activities improve the performance of investee companies. But there is a fairly general belief that investment managers have not performed well in terms of promoting good governance and stewardship, and delivering good returns to savers as a result. The returns received by savers over recent years have been low and transaction costs have been enormous. The annual inflation-adjusted return on UK pension funds between 1963 and 1999 was 5.0 per cent, but averaged only around 1.1 per cent between 2000 and 2009. At the same time, transaction costs have been enormous, with the financial sector taking for itself some 40 per cent of all corporate profits in the years before the 2008 financial crash, and bankers paying themselves huge bonuses.

How has this situation come about? A major reason is the increased fragmentation of the shareholdings of UK equities. Fifty years ago, most shares in the UK were held by individuals who were advised by stockbrokers who had direct knowledge of both their clients and the companies in which they invested. Today, individual shareholders, excluding holdings in nominee accounts, own 11 per cent of UK equities (including these holdings, the figure is thought to be closer to 20 per cent). The holdings of pension funds and insurance companies now account for around 14 per cent of the total, and the proportion attributed to non-UK holders is over 40 per cent. This fragmentation has reduced the incentives for engagement and the level of control enjoyed by each shareholder. At the same time, there has been a massive growth in the amount of intermediation in equity investment, driven both by a desire for greater professionalism and efficiency and by a decline in trust and confidence in the investment chain. Between the saver and the company, we now find trustees, investment consultants, managers who allocate funds to specialist asset managers, and investment managers who have become the key agent in the investment chain. This growth of intermediation has led to increased costs for investors, and an increased potential for misaligned incentives.

This situation, in which investment managers cream off large sums of money from the returns which flow from companies to savers and pay themselves large bonuses, cannot be allowed to continue. But what can be done to reverse it? One course of action would be for policymakers to attempt to regulate the behaviour of investment managers. But, as Paul Woolley has argued, bankers will strongly resist and actively seek to get around such regulations, which in any case it would be difficult to construct. Instead, he suggests that a better way would be to encourage the giant funds, such as the large pension, sovereign wealth, charitable and endowment funds around the world, to act to stop it. But it will take more than action by the giant funds to bring about the necessary changes. What is disgraceful is the way that savers generally have been exploited by investment managers, and this appropriation of wealth will only be stopped when all savers take action to force investment managers to behave differently, and to act on behalf of investors and not on behalf of themselves. In other words, we need to make our financial system work as it is supposed to work in a capitalist economy. The new Shareholders Advisory Board, which it was proposed be established to improve corporate governance should have an important role to play here.

UK equity markets are no longer a significant source of funding for new investment by UK companies but this does not mean that the problem of providing equity capital to small and medium-sized companies is no longer an issue. There are plenty of examples of high-tech firms wanting to grow and capable of competing in world markets, and we need to reform our financial system so that it provides them with the funds they need to grow and be profitable.

FURTHER DISCUSSION OF WHAT NEEDS TO BE DONE

The set of interlocking institutional arrangements in the finance sector that allowed the crash to happen and helped to tip the economy into its deepest recession since the 1930s remain largely intact.

The financial system needs to change and government needs to do more to bring this about. But there are limits to the role regulation can play and non-financial companies, savers and investors need to alter their behaviour too in order to force financial institutions to reform themselves.

There are many aspects to the underperformance of the financial sector and much that needs to change. Broadly speaking, four steps are required to improve its performance: banks have to be made more boring by making them safer; alternative forms of finance to bank lending have to be found for small and medium-sized firms; rent extraction needs to be reduced, particularly in the asset management industry; and the ultimate owners of capital have to become more engaged with what happens to their money.

Making Banks Safer

Failings in the banking system were at the heart of the financial crash of 2008, though its root cause lay elsewhere. Central banks in developed economies kept interest rates too low in the mid-2000s. They chose to ignore rapid rates of credit growth, focusing instead on consumer price inflation and their guesses about the amount of spare capacity in their economies. Because they did not see any inflationary pressures in consumer markets, monetary policies were kept easy, even when capital from emerging economies began flooding into their economies and asset prices started to rise rapidly. The result in many economies, including the US and the UK, was very high borrowing and a massive housing bubble. It was the bursting of this bubble in the US in 2007 that led to the financial crash.

This crash was on a scale not seen since the 1930s because of developments in the banking system that fuelled the growth of credit in the economy. Ultimately, given the consequences, there were serious misjudgements on the part of senior executives in the financial industry. But there was also a failure of regulation. Banks were allowed to take risks on a scale that should not have been allowed.

In future, the banking system should be more boring, with banks that behave more like utilities and are less likely to fail.

Change is necessary because banks have become too big to fail, resulting in a socialisation of risk. In good times, buoyant income results in high levels of remuneration and profits for the industry, but, in bad times, banks have to be bailed out by the taxpayer. Insiders can receive massive rewards without bearing proportionate risks. The large banks in the UK act as they do because the government provides an implicit insurance policy for their activities. By promising to bail them out of any crisis, the government is, in effect, subsidising their cost of capital and encouraging them to take on excessive levels of risk and debt. Reducing this implicit subsidy requires action to lower the chance of future crises and to create mechanisms for re-capitalising or winding up failed banks in a way that minimises future taxpayer liabilities. This is particularly pertinent for the UK because the presence of large international banks here means UK taxpayers are in effect subsidising global banking.

The best solution for the UK would be an international agreement on mechanisms for dealing with a failing bank. But getting enough countries to cooperate on such a deal appears unlikely. This is despite some steps having been taken to reduce the risks of another crash – in particular, Basel III regulations that oblige banks to hold higher capital reserves. Domestically, the authorities have not been idle: retail and investment banking activities are to be ring-fenced and banks are creating 'living wills'. However, these steps are insufficient and further action is needed to protect taxpayers. This might include stricter caps on leverage, as proposed by the Vickers Commission, and changes in the tax system to remove the favourable tax treatment of debt compared to equity.

Banks also need to be made more boring by ensuring that they treat their stakeholders fairly. A number of large-scale abuses of banks' customers have taken place over the last decade, including the fixing of LIBOR rates, the mis-selling of payment protection insurance and the mis-selling of inappropriate derivative products to small firms. Responsibility for protecting customers from abuse lies with boards and the senior management of financial institutions, but they should be held to account by their shareholders who ultimately pay the price when scandals and fines lower share prices. However, when management and boards have so obviously failed in their duties and shareholders have failed to hold them to account, the government has had to step in to ensure compensation to those affected by past abuses. It has also established the Financial Conduct Authority and instructed it to reduce the risk of further abuses, though only time will tell how effective it will be in protecting banks' customers in the future and whether further action is needed.

Finding Alternative Sources of Finance for Small and Medium-Sized Firms

Safer, more boring banks might lend more to UK businesses, but their lending is unlikely ever to be sufficient to meet demand in full. The financial sector's primary role is to allocate capital in the most efficient manner but there are parts of the economy, such as small businesses, that are starved of the capital they need, despite lending within the financial services industry reaching extraordinary levels. Ninety per cent of outstanding loans are currently for either financial or property deals.

This suggests the credit system is creating too much of the wrong sort of debt, with profound negative implications for the economy. Excessive lending within the financial system and to the housing market causes unsustainable asset price inflation and macroeconomic instability, while insufficient lending to the 'real economy' hinders the creation of long-term, sustainable growth. The remit of the Financial Policy Committee (FPC) of the Bank of England should be amended to include a mandate to guide the quantity and type of credit in the economy. This would go beyond the powers to intervene in the housing market that have recently been requested by the FPC, which involve limiting loan-to-value and loan-to-income multiples.

Large companies are largely self-financing, as they are able to fund investment and expansion from their cash flow. They are also in a position to issue debt – in the form of corporate bonds – when they need additional funds, and are incentivised by the tax system to favour debt over equity. Traditionally, banks have been the major source of funding for small and medium-sized firms in the UK. The relatively small number of UK companies that access the new issue market do so predominantly to repay early-stage investors or private equity investors rather than to raise funds for investment. There have, however, been long-standing concerns about the level of funding, particularly long-term funding, provided by banks, dating back at least to the Macmillan Report of 1931 (hence the problem is often known as the 'Macmillan gap').

The Macmillan gap still exists today. Although the recession caused a drop in demand for funding, the recovery will mean more small and medium-sized firms seeking to grow. It is important that a lack of finance does not hold them back, but there is no prospect of banks being able to meet demand for borrowing as it increases in coming years. Banks are reluctant to invest the time and money needed to assess the quality of small and medium-sized firms' proposals and the attendant risks. Instead, they adopt a 'tick-box' approach that makes it hard – even impossible – for firms with little track record or limited collateral to get the funds they need.

The government should step in to fill the gap in funding. The externalities that accrue to the wider economy from the existence of a vibrant small and medium-sized company sector justify action. The Business Growth Fund, Business Bank and Green Investment Bank are not on the scale required. The government should establish a larger state investment bank to ensure that small and medium-sized companies can get the finance they need. This bank should operate like the Industrial and Commercial Finance Corporation, which was established in 1945 by the Bank of England and leading banks, setting up local branches and employing staff with expertise across industrial sectors. This will ensure that it can make good investments across the whole of the economy.

Any state investment bank should be 100 per cent state-owned. It should be profit-making – though not necessarily profit-maximising – but it should not pay a dividend. Profits should be ploughed back into the bank to allow it to further increase its lending. The government would have to provide the new bank with its initial capital, which would be a problem given the constraints on the public finances. One option would be to instruct the Bank of England to do another round of quantitative easing specifically for this purpose. Alternatively, the funds would have to be found by cutting other spending, increased taxation, the sale of government assets or extra borrowing.

Reducing Rent Extraction in Banking

Rent extraction is rife in the financial sector. Finance represents a much bigger share of the economy in the UK than it did 30 years ago, prior to the 'Big Bang' of deregulation. Some of this growth reflects the success of the industry in increasing its share of the global market in financial services, but much is in domestic markets and there is no evidence that it has led to capital being allocated more efficiently, higher investment returns or lower capital costs. The financial sector has grown because it is extracting larger rents from the rest of the economy. This is a cause for concern because rents extracted by finance are equivalent to a tax on the rest of the economy (rather than the cost of the provision of useful services), diminishing its ability to invest and grow.

One manifestation of the extraordinary level of rent extraction in the UK is the scale of pay and bonuses in finance, which have increased massively over the last three decades despite no improvement in returns to customers. These excess wages do not accrue to the average worker; they are concentrated among the highest earners in finance, adding to income inequality. Before the financial crash, there was little questioning of pay and bonuses, which were misread as signs of the sector's success. This illusion should have been shattered in 2008, but high pay and bonuses have survived, suggesting the degree of rent extraction remains very large.

The case for an attack on rent-seeking behaviour is compelling, but finding the right response is not easy. It should, though, include measures to increase transparency and competition. Transparency – maximising the information available to all participants – makes markets work better, but only if there is sufficient competition. Rent-seekers exploit monopoly and quasi-monopoly conditions; competition minimises their opportunities.

The conditions that make rent extraction easy – high-concentration, barriers to entry and a lack of pricing transparency – have all been present in the UK's retail banking sector for some time. Challenger banks, actions to lower barriers to entry, making it easier for consumers to switch banks and increased transparency on fees and charges have only made a small difference to the situation. Further steps will be necessary to create real competition in retail banking. Governments might baulk at the idea of breaking up the existing banks, even those in which the public owns a large stake, but ultimately greater competition requires the existing large retail banks to have much smaller shares of the market.

While increasing competition in the UK retail financial sector is a worthy goal, most rent extraction occurs elsewhere in the financial sector: in corporate banking, investment banking and proprietary trading. Large corporations pay inflated fees, larger spreads, and higher interest rates and other charges than they would in a truly competitive market.

Measures to address rent extraction from corporate clients are not obvious or likely to be simple. More regulation is probably not the answer because it just encourages evasion. Ultimately, the culture of banks has to be changed. Rent extraction increased significantly with the shift to a transactional, short-term, trading culture at many banks starting in the 1980s. At present, large investment banks exist primarily to maximise the salaries, bonuses and share options of their staff rather than to deliver the best possible service to their customers and counterparties. Banks have to be made to re-adopt a culture that values long-term relationships and emphasises their duty of care towards their clients. However, there is little to suggest the incumbents of the City have experienced a moral revolution since the financial crash, or that they are about to do so in the future.

Reducing Rent Extraction in Investment Management

Rent extraction also occurs on a large scale in the investment management industry. Investment managers, in particular, skim off a large percentage of the returns investors should be getting from companies. Furthermore, the growth of intermediation has created a huge principal-agent problem. There is an information asymmetry working against investors, who do not know how competent and diligent their agents will be, and misaligned incentives because the interests of all the parties involved are not necessarily aligned with those of the investor.

Active asset management in the equity market (as opposed to passively matching the index) is almost a zero-sum game. In aggregate, active managers can only produce returns in excess of the market return – before taking account of fees and other costs – by outperforming other investors in the market – principally individual holders of stocks. But the share of the market held by these other investors has shrunk so much that there is now little scope for this to happen. As a result, active managers as a group do not perform better than passive managers before fees and costs are taken into account, and perform less well once they are.

It is only possible, therefore, to justify the existence of active asset managers if their activities improve the performance of the companies they invest in – to the benefit of the economy as a whole and of savers who will receive higher returns. However, they have failed in this respect as well because they take too short term a view. Asset managers have become traders rather than investors, focused on their quarterly and annual performance rather than on long-term returns. Their portfolios are turned over frequently and their level of engagement with companies is low. They are less concerned with good governance and stewardship than with short-term earnings per share.

This is a widely held view, but it has not triggered a significant change in behaviour among investors. While some investors choose to invest in relatively cheap passive funds, others are still chasing higher returns from active managers, including hedge funds and private equity funds. This is despite the high and one-sided fee structures employed by these funds, including performance fees for outperformance but no deduction for underperformance. The implicit coordination of hedge fund and private equity fee structures also allows funds to extract rents from their clients. Most firms in these sectors charge their institutional clients a fee equal to 2 per cent of the assets under management plus a 20 per cent share of any investment gains over a specified benchmark. Some firms justify these fees with outstanding performance, but many do not and still get rich at the expense of their clients. Large institutional investors could perhaps push back against such practices and secure lower fees, though not all choose to do so, but small investors have little choice but to pay up if they want to invest in these asset classes.

There is no incentive for the asset management industry to change; the status quo is in their interests. Investment managers are more than happy to capture excessive rents by encouraging complexity and opacity over charges, milking their customers by offering them false promises of high returns. Financial innovation has been rife in the last 20 years and there are now large markets in financial instruments such as credit default swaps (CDS) and collateralised debt obligations (CDOs), and huge sums of money invested in private equity and hedge funds. These innovations have clearly benefited the investment banks and fund managers through high fees and charges. It is less clear that, in aggregate, they have benefited investors.

Urging Investors to Take a New Approach

Regulating the pace of financial innovation can only do so much to prevent rent extraction; investors need to change. Investors, particularly large investors like pension funds, insurance companies and endowment trusts, need to take back greater control of their assets and force their investment managers to act differently. This will require a change of attitude on their part. The trend for investment managers to be increasingly short term in their outlook has been driven as much by investors requiring their managers to perform on an annual, or even a quarterly, basis – and changing them if they do not – as it has by the investment managers themselves. The only way to break out of a position where everyone's focus has become so short term is for investors to adopt a new approach.

Individual savers into pension funds should have a right to know how their money is being invested: what investment policy is being pursued and why it is judged to be the best approach to delivering long-term returns. They should also be informed about the activities of their fund's investment managers in engaging with companies to deliver long-term value. And they should be able to formally question investment policies.

Investors should only appoint investment managers who use a long-term, value-based method when investing that takes into account issues such as environmental sustainability. They should also place a cap on the turnover of their portfolios and insist on full disclosure of fees and charges. And they should judge performance (and pay performance fees) only over long periods of time. It is in their best interests to do so – but then it has been for many years and they have proved reluctant to act.

For this reason, the government should play a part too, though not through regulation of investment managers because they will seek to evade it. The government should make clear in law that pension trustees are not obliged to seek to maximise short-term returns, while ignoring wider considerations. It should also establish a body to support and advise investors on their relationships with their investment managers. This body – a Shareholders Advisory Board – would require real powers to hold investment managers to account, including requiring them to set out clearly and fully the fees and other charges they make. It should also work directly with large investors and indirectly with smaller ones (through, for example, the National Association of Pension Funds) to bring about a change in what they ask of their investment managers. Long-term investors should require their investment managers to be similarly long term in their investment strategies, placing more emphasis on the fundamental value of the companies that they invest in and less on their short-term profits. Investors should also use their power directly as shareholders and indirectly through their investment managers to encourage companies to adopt long-term policies that enhance their value.

CONCLUSION

A modern economy cannot function without a healthy financial sector. From the point of view of the industry, the UK's financial sector is in rude health: it has grown large relative to the rest of the economy, makes huge profits and pays high salaries and bonuses. It is also a major source of overseas income. However, from the point of view of the rest of the economy, things look rather different: taxpayers subsidise the financial sector and have had to bail it out of crises; small firms cannot get the funds they need to expand; and the sector's customers pay high fees and charges but receive poor returns, and pay a higher cost for capital.

The challenge for policymakers and for customers of the financial sector is to find a way to make it deliver a better service to the rest of the economy at a lower cost. Government has a part to play – for example, through regulation that increases transparency – but its actions will have limited effect without action on the part of firms, savers and investors. Ultimately, they are the ones that are losing out as a result of the extensive rent-seeking behaviour of the financial sector, and they are the ones that have to force it to change.

THE POLITICAL CHALLENGE OF PROGRESSIVE CAPITALISM

Roger Liddle and Patrick Diamond

Among the most insistent questions in British politics is what model of capitalism the UK needs to remain a wealthy and cohesive society in the wake of the 2008 financial crash. Since the economic crisis, public disquiet about avaricious global capitalism has been palpable. The UK suffered its worst recession since the second world war and the subsequent economic recovery has lagged behind those in other major economies. But even now that growth has picked up and output has overtaken pre-crises levels, wages have stagnated and the productivity shortfall between the UK and the G7 economies is at its biggest for more than 20 years. The growing unpopularity of business and large corporations risks undermining the implicit moral contract in favour of open markets. The backlash against the private sector is hardly surprising: when financial institutions broke down following the collapse of Lehman Brothers in 2008, the costs fell not on wealthy financiers but on society as a whole, at a time when middle-income households were suffering an unprecedented squeeze in their living standards.

The irony is that *both* bankers and the left have faltered in the wake of the crash. Neoliberals have argued that the crisis was the product of government failure – and that the state should be immediately reined in. Far from gaining politically from the 'crisis of capitalism', the left has been profoundly disorientated. The New Labour model of political economy, having pledged allegiance both to Thatcherite deregulated markets and an overly complacent social democratic model of 'tax and spend', was shaken to its core. Despite delivering 44 consecutive quarters of real GDP growth, Labour's embrace of neoliberalism in the 1990s ultimately guaranteed neither economic stability nor the sound productive base necessary to sustain long-term social investment.

NEW LABOUR'S LEGACY

The Blair/Brown economic legacy was one of under-investment in key infrastructure, notably transport and energy; a continuing decline in the share of manufacturing in the economy contributing to a structural balance of payments deficit exacerbated by an overvalued pound; an accelerating regional economic divide; and a speculative property and construction boom financing public and private consumption through high levels of government and household debt.

However, not everything about the pre-2008 model was proved wrong. Research, innovation and high-tech start-ups flourished; the scale of government investment in science and technology was unprecedented; labour market flexibility generally kept unemployment down; Britain's cities underwent a renaissance; and the United Kingdom remained a successful base for global companies. The challenge for progressive capitalism is to build on these gains while addressing the underlying structural weaknesses of an unbalanced economy: low productivity and weak balance of payments. These weaknesses limit Britain's productive potential, thereby accentuating the long tail of inequality that has become a pronounced characteristic of advanced economies over the last 30 years. More than that, progressive thinkers must espouse a practical vision of an inclusive capitalism around which an enduring public settlement can be built.

THE ENABLING STATE IN A GLOBALISED ECONOMY

As John Maynard Keynes foresaw in the 1920s, the debate about progressive capitalism concerns the 'agenda' and 'non-agenda' of government. Governments should do only what is not being done adequately by markets. However, market failure extends well beyond conventional areas of supply-side intervention in the economy, such as skills, science and research. A short-term business culture in Britain prevents firms from nurturing new products and services. Why does so much technological innovation originate in Britain, but so few start-ups grow into world-beating high-tech companies? Too few small and medium-sized enterprises can access finance for growth. Why does Britain have fewer micro businesses than any comparable industrial economy? Despite its financial services sophistication, why does the City seem systemically incapable of channelling savings into long-term projects that enhance Britain's productive potential beyond London and the south-east? Too few sectors are actively championed as beacons of national success. Why do French, German and Scandinavian governments celebrate national companies, but British governments generally do not?

A progressive capitalism can only be forged by an enabling state that understands the global environment in which today's business leaders operate: where survival depends on profitability, where the world is awash with investment opportunities beyond the UK, and where arbitrary interventions in markets and constant changes in government policy discourage the long-term investment Britain needs. Businesses that act against the public interest should not escape regulatory action, but it is not the job of governments to pick and choose between 'predators' and 'responsible' capitalists. Nor is it sensible to treat smaller firms as inherently more virtuous than larger ones: what matters is setting a stable policy framework in which making a reasonable profit is compatible with the public interest. It makes no sense to be anti-business when the vast majority of the UK workforce is employed in the private sector. It remains correct to support a flourishing market economy to generate the fruits of growth to invest in a dynamic public realm.

INTELLECTUAL ROOTS

The search for a progressive capitalism has a long history drawing on venerable intellectual traditions. Some of the most imaginative and critical thinking has come from within the private sector, as well as from academics, policymakers, civil society, and faith communities. Ideas have also emerged on the right as well as the left of the political spectrum concerning the failings of modern capitalism and markets. The most prominent exponent of this view is the London School of Economics' political theorist John Gray, who was once himself a vociferous advocate of the Thatcher revolution. Gray has highlighted the hubris of neoliberalism for ignoring the importance of a culture of the common good in sustaining and nurturing market institutions.

The second strand of thought on progressive capitalism is the tradition of 'stakeholder capitalism', epitomised by Will Hutton, alongside writers such as John Kay and John Plender. Their ideas have developed in response to the failings of free market economics. Kay, Hutton and Plender are strong critics of shareholder short-termism and Britain's takeover culture. They argue that investment managers should exercise duties of stewardship, rather than maximising short-term returns; companies should serve the interests of a wider group of stakeholders, not only shareholders; and successful businesses are rooted in their communities, acknowledging wider social obligations.

A third related strand is the critique of 'shareholder value' promulgated by the American business guru, Michael Porter. In a recent article in the *Harvard Business Review*, Porter argued of today's capitalism, "A big part of the problem lies with companies themselves, which remain trapped in an outdated approach to value creation that has emerged over the past few decades." Porter attests that the private sector continues to conceive value creation too narrowly.

The emphasis on optimising short-term financial performance ensures the most important customer needs are underplayed. Moreover, the broader influences that determine long-term business success, from high-quality infrastructure to social inclusion, are too often ignored. "Companies must take the lead in bringing business and society back together," Porter counsels.

NEW INDUSTRIAL ACTIVISM

Defining a model of inclusive prosperity and progressive capitalism that treats business as part of the solution rather than the problem ought to be at the forefront of a social democratic approach to economic policy. The challenge is to position the active state and responsible ownership as essential prerequisites of business success in an age of intensive global competition.

The gap social democrats must fill in their view of political economy is two-fold. First, they must flesh out the substance of the effective developmental state Britain failed to create in the aftermath of the second world war, using public power to promote national competitiveness in a world of cut-throat competition. Previous attempts at industrial activism failed because the British state was ill-equipped to actively shape and steer markets, having its roots in a 19th century liberal laissez-faire state that was inimical to public intervention. A developmental state entails the step-by-step creation of new national institutions, building on the successful Technology Strategy Board and the spread of new Catapult centres which are helping to turn research breakthroughs into commercially marketable products.

Second, the Treasury blind-spot about not lending to business is unsustainable if UK private banks are not in a position to provide finance for growth. Almost every government in Europe owns a credit institution that can make long-term loans to growing companies, helping innovators through the 'valley of death' between developing a product and profitable sales. We need new publicly guaranteed mechanisms for supplying patient 'equity' so that successful entrepreneurs do not 'cash in' at the first available opportunity, but stay the course to build successful companies with a potentially global reach. The aversion to risking public money in order to back British growth companies has to be reversed. Such activism is viewed as too derivative of 1970s-style 'picking winners', but at the same time it is acceptable for public policy to artificially inflate the housing market.

A MORE INCLUSIVE CAPITALISM

A progressive capitalism entails a reformed state where power is not hoarded in Whitehall and Westminster but dispersed throughout the nations and regions of Britain. At the same time, vocational qualifications and apprenticeship standards need to be simplified and made more rigorous through independent national bodies, with a greater role for professional institutes. The funding of high-level apprenticeships, particularly in the fields of science, technology, engineering and maths, has to be a partnership between public funders and employers from the bottom-up.

A major task in forging a new political economy is to secure the backing of business for a model of inclusive capitalism that restores public confidence in the moral virtue of wealth creation where doing well, and properly paying taxes due, is seen to be of societal, as well as private, benefit. There is the potential to win the backing of a new generation of entrepreneurs whose business success depends on building partnerships throughout their company with committed and highly trained staff, and developing long-term relationships with their customer-base. Any viable project to fashion a progressive capitalism needs a new model of the firm. Companies may not want to follow the model of the John Lewis Partnership, but its success demonstrates that there are alternatives to the conventional limited liability company that should be actively encouraged. We need a step-change in employee ownership throughout the British economy, ensuring that wealth is dispersed into many more hands.

There is a new dialogue to be opened up between business and the centre left about what kind of modern welfare state a vibrant progressive capitalism needs. The downside for individuals in a dynamic, innovating economy is that the rapidity of technological change threatens incumbent companies, making skills redundant and destroying jobs in ways no one can presently foresee. Just as the NHS was founded on the principle that no one can have perfect knowledge of whether they will enjoy good health in the future, and therefore collective insurance is the most equitable solution, social security needs to be re-thought for an age of ever more rapid economic change, as individuals seek more choice around how to balance work and family life.

A progressive capitalism needs long-term investment in infrastructure and productive assets through new approaches to financing public services. It requires world-class health and education, with investment in skills, science, knowledge and innovation. And it must be complemented by a fairer distribution of capital and assets, with an 'ownership revolution' that locates control over wealth throughout society instead of narrowly rewarding the existing political and economic elite.

The aims of a progressive political economy ought to be forging a resilient and balanced economy where people and businesses can plan ahead; delivering more egalitarian outcomes that narrow the inequalities of wealth and ownership that characterise modern capitalist economies; and sustaining growth that is necessary both for rising living standards and improvements in public services.

The danger of globalisation is that it will amplify the gaps between the 'winners' and 'losers' of change, creating a permanently marginalised minority with little stake in the nation's future. The aim of economic policy must be to create balanced and sustainable growth to improve the living standards of those on lower and middle incomes while ensuring that Britain grows together. It requires genuine partnership between the public and private sectors where the state actively invests in economic potential.

FILLING THE VOID

No party has yet succeeded in filling the void in Britain's political economy that opened up in 2008 between the emphasis on central planning and nationalisation, a policy applied between 1945 and 1979, and the market liberal laissez-faire approach pursued in Britain ever since. The ideas around progressive capitalism offer the opportunity to define a more robust and substantial prospectus for the British centre left. Social democracy wins the battle of ideas when it projects an uplifting, optimistic vision of Britain's future: a conception of national modernisation allied to a vision of social fairness. Ironically, just at the point when some doubt whether government has any future, it has never been more necessary in fashioning a new economic model for the post-crisis age.

Patrick Diamond is vice-chair of Policy Network and lecturer in public policy at Queen Mary, University of London.

Roger Liddle is chair of Policy Network and a member of the House of Lords.